Contents

This cover has been designed using resources from Freepik.com.

Elementor + WordPress Book

Welcome to *the* book on building a WordPress website with Elementor. This book is created by Isotropic Design, a leading agency on the East Coast that builds responsive WordPress websites and offers numerous other digital services. Since 2017, Isotropic has been building websites with Elementor and WordPress. In that time, we've become well versed in both tools and created this book to share our knowledge with you. We noticed that there's a lot of demand for a simple guide on creating a WordPress website with Elementor – that's why we wrote this book.

When it comes to building a website, working with a digital agency is a good option in many cases. If you're looking to build a super functional and customized site, utilizing an agency allows you to access talent, scale, and pricing that is beneficial to your company. At the same time, local small businesses may not be able to afford a completely customized agency website and are looking to build something themselves.

If you're in that customer group, somebody looking to build their own website that is responsive, good-looking, and professional, then this book is for you. In this guide you're going to learn how to create a website using WordPress and Elementor from the ground up.

If you have any questions about building a WordPress website with Elementor, feel free to reach out to the team at Isotropic Design via our Facebook Page. We would be happy to help you answer any questions and aid in any way we can.

What This Book Is

Before we get into the actual content of this book, we wanted to discuss what you can expect out of it. We believe in transparency across all our business divisions and bring that mentality to our writing as well.

This book is created to be a solid reference guide that will point you in the right direction when building a website from scratch using Elementor and WordPress. You can expect to be pointed to many different guides, products, and more that will help you to build a good digital presence for you and your small business.

We're going to walk you through everything that goes into making a website. We feel that we are qualified to discuss this because our main business is website creation, and in the many years that we've been doing it, we've isolated individual services, products, workflows, and more that results in a very efficient way of creating websites. In this guide, we're going to share everything that we've learned with you regarding website creation with WordPress, Elementor and a collection of third-party tools.

The target audience of this book is somebody who wants to build a website but has limited technical experience and knowledge. Our example website is on that is built for a local small business, but you can apply the principles discussed in the book to any Elementor website project, large or small.

Building your own website allows you to customize it as you want, while also saving you the cost of going through a digital agency. If you're a small business with a small marketing budget, doing it yourself can be extremely impactful by developing a personalized online presence that helps with search engine ranking placement, local SEO marketing, and more. As an agency, we feel that any business needs a website in 2020.

Overall, **81%** of Americans say they go online daily, and most consumers in the United States will check for you online before purchasing your product or service. Having a well-designed website that effectively conveys information makes your business more credible and will lead to increased revenue.

We're going to walk you through our favorite website structure for small businesses and outline specific principles that are essential to creating a successful website.

If you design the website correctly, it will serve as a lead generator (on autopilot) for years to come.

What This Book Is Not

As we stated a couple paragraphs ago, this book is going to point you to products, guides, services, and methods that will help you build a website.

This book is not an all-in-one guide on everything to do with WordPress and Elementor, as that would be impossible to contain in one single publication. For example, we're not going to walk you through every aspect of the Elementor page builder (like coloring buttons or creating video backgrounds). What we are going to do is point you to essential guides and resources that will help you do this and teach you with the information you need to go from nothing to a fully functional website in 2020.

One of the greatest things about WordPress and Elementor, and something that we're going to go into more depth about in a few sections of this book, is the community that surrounds them. There's an amazing support community, with a ton of 3rd party free resources like YouTube videos that will help you do anything you want on either of the platforms.

So, instead of telling you how exactly to build the website, we're going to arm you with the tools and knowledge that you need to effectively create your own personalized website.

As many say, having the right tool will only bring you so far. Understanding how to use that tool properly will help you build whatever you want. That's what this book is going to teach you to do. It's going to connect you to the proper tools, teach you how to use them and connect you to additional educational resources should you need any more info.

Introduction

What Is WordPress

Self-hosted WordPress is the most popular content management system and website builder in the universe. 35%+ of all websites online use WordPress as their underlying framework. To put that in perspective, there are 500 websites created every minute, and there are 1.5 billion websites that are live right now.

This platform is free, search engine optimized, user-friendly, secure, immensely expandable, and known as the gold standard when it comes to website building for everybody from a local small business to Fortune 500 companies. Here are a few sites that use WordPress:

- The New York Post
- BBC
- Swell Bottles
- AMC Networks

The competitors to WordPress are known brands like Squarespace, Wix, and Weebly. Each company offers a website builder, but when compared to WordPress, they're much more limited and higher priced. If you're reading this book, we'll assume that you have already chosen to use WordPress as your content management system and website building framework, so we won't go in depth into why we think WordPress is a much better choice than any other website builder out there.

[Though if you need more context, take a look at these resources:

- https://kinsta.com/blog/wordpress-site-examples
- https://capsicummediaworks.com/why-wordpress-is-the-best-cms/   ]

There are some things to understand when it comes to WordPress. This book is going to refer to the free, open source version of WordPress, which can be found at wordpress.org. Like most open source projects, there's a paid solution that is built upon the open source code. With WordPress, that paid solution can be found at wordpress.com. You don't want to be using this platform because it's very limiting, and created specifically for small, personal bloggers.

Wordpress.org offers all of the same functionalities that Wordpress.com offers, but the reason it's free is because you need to set it up and hosted yourself. This is standard throughout all open source projects.

With Wordpress.com, if you want all of the features that the open source self-hosted version of WordPress offers, you would need to pay $5000 per month for hosting plus a $5000 setup fee. This service is called the WordPress VIP and is oriented towards Fortune 500 companies (though we don't understand why this is a viable offering when you can self host WordPress and get many more features for much less -- Even if you're a company that requires immense hosting and processing power behind your website).

Building Blocks Of WordPress: Plugins & Themes

WordPress has two building blocks. These individual building blocks allow creators to build whatever they want on the platform. For example, if a company wants a job board, they can build that with WordPress using a specific plugin and theme set. If the company wants a video streaming platform, they can do that as well with a different set of themes and plugins.

What Are Plugins? (Building Block #1)

WordPress plugins add immense functionality to your website. There are 50,000 free plugins on the WordPress repository that allow you to do pretty much anything you want with your website. For example, if you need to collect entries, there are tons of free and paid form plugins out there. If you need a slider to display content visually in your website, there's a bunch of plugins to do that as well.

With plugins, there are free and premium solutions. In many circumstances, free plugins work very well, and in other circumstances paid plugins do the job much better.

What Are Themes? (Building Block #2)

You can think about WordPress themes as a package that adds a specific design to your WordPress website. While you can change the underlying content within the theme, the theme dictates the actual design and styling of the website. There are also free and paid themes, but typically the free themes are extremely limited, while the paid themes offer a lot more (for $).

Especially with themes, there are some limitations. Because themes typically change the appearance of the website, you are somewhat limited to what the developers create. You can think about a theme as an Instagram filter. You can change the underlying structure of the photo that has an Instagram filter applied to it, but you can't change the overall look of the photo when the filter's applied. That is the same as a theme. You can change the structure, content, and images under the theme, but websites that use the same themes typically look very similar.

With traditional themes, you are offered a collection of page designs that you are required to use. These individual designs are maybe for a service page, or an about page, or a blog post. However, you are required to use the templates that come with the theme, and can't really customize them without advanced knowledge in PHP, CSS, and HTML.

The best themes are always paid, rightfully so. Developers spend a lot of time when it comes to creating good themes for WordPress, which means that all of them are paid solutions. Themes will typically cost you anywhere from $40 to $300 (per year if you want ongoing updates & support). A big issue that many small business owners have when it comes to purchasing themes is that they need to rely on the individual developer for support. They need to use the given styling, which is hard to customize if you don't have knowledge in programming and coding, and spending $300 on a theme and discovering that it doesn't work for you isn't fun.

Traditionally, those who are creating WordPress websites will pair a good theme and a collection of plugins together to create their final product. As an agency, we may sometimes develop custom themes that allow our clients to do whatever they want with their website. Keep in mind that these custom themes have the same limitations mentioned above; we will create a set amount of page templates that our customers will be required to use. However, at least when working with an agency, the client can dictate the styling of the templates as we build them.

If you are looking for a completely custom, advanced solution, this book may not be for you. While WordPress and Elementor will allow you to build whatever you want, you may need advanced knowledge in CSS, HTML, and PHP to create the exact functionality that you're looking for. Before you continue in this book, think about what you're trying to do. Sometimes it's best to work with a professional who knows how to create custom solutions, rather then trying to do it yourself.

You always need to determine if the time you're going to spend creating something is worth it, or if you want to pay somebody else to create it for you. If that somebody else can use their time more efficiently than you, then it's worth considering working with somebody else and taking the role of delegator, not creator. However, if you're in our target readership, which is a small business owner looking for a simple digital presence, then continue with his book as we will be teaching you how to create an awesome website using WordPress, Elementor, and not much else.

What Is Elementor

The simplest description of Elementor we can give you is that it is a **theme builder**. Theme builders (we may refer to theme builders as page builders, in this book, they're the same thing) allow you to visually create website pages, templates, headers, and footers using a graphical user interface. Essentially, they offer you a user interface that will generate HTML and CSS, without you actually needing to know HTML and CSS.

Think back to the limitations that we discussed when reviewing the two essential building blocks of WordPress, plugins and themes. The main limitations were that you were trapped using the specific designs of a theme and everything good costs a pretty penny. If you wanted to customize the theme too completely fit your branding, design, and style, it would be difficult to do this unless you had knowledge in CSS and HTML. So, for an example, if you wanted to build a services page, you would have to use a set template to do so. If you wanted to make any changes to this individual services page, it would be difficult to do so outside of the confines of the theme.

Elementor allows you to build any page, theme, header, and more using a visual page builder. So, instead of needing to know advanced HTML, CSS, and PHP, all you need is a good eye for design, and a good guide on getting started. Once you understand how to use Elementor, you can really build anything you want.

The Elementor page builder comes pre packaged with over 100 individual elements that you can use to build website pages. These elements range from structural components like sections, columns, and buttons, to images, to tabs, to forms and more.

You build individual pages by dragging and dropping elements onto a canvas.

Elementor Brings Powerful features to Everyday Users

Elementor replaces the traditional building blocks of WordPress. Instead of using a premade theme, you can build your own theme to your exact specifications. This means you can create a great web presence for your business that is completely customized to your needs. You can do this visually, meaning you don't need to know any code, and you don't need to have any advanced knowledge in web development.

The Elementor page builder is revolutionary when it comes to WordPress development, and has completely changed the industry. Previously, you would need to contract with a web designer to create a completely custom, good-looking website. Now, all you need is to get a good collection of plugins, Elementor, hosting, and a good guide (that's what this is) to build the website yourself.

When it comes to plugins, Elementor replaces the need for many of them. For example, if you wanted a slider with a traditional theme, you would probably have to go ahead and purchase a plugin that allowed you to visually build sliders. If you wanted forms, you would need to go ahead and use a free or paid solution to add the form functionality to your website.

Elementor took the basic requirements for any website and included them in their page builder. Now, instead of needing to go ahead and purchase a slider plugin, they've included that functionality in their page builder.

Instead of needing to go ahead and purchase forms, they've included a form builder in their solution.

An extremely powerful function that isn't usually mentioned when it comes to Elementor is its pop-up builder. It allows you to visually create popups, and assign rules to them (for example, the popup would show on the user's exit intent) without the need for any third-party plugin. Previously, the best third-party plugin on the market that allowed you to visually build popups and offered the same triggering criteria as elementary cost $79 per year.

Despite being so powerful, Elementor works alongside WordPress and is installed as a traditional plug-in.

The tool will also easily integrate with existing plugins. For example, if you need more functionality than what the base page builder offers, which is usually the case if you're trying to build a website that is specifically customized to meet the needs of your company, you would still need to go ahead and get a plugin to add that functionality.

To summarize this section, Elementor allows you to do things that were previously only possible through custom CSS, HTML, and PHP coding. It was only a few years ago that to access the customization that element or allows you to do , you would need to build a custom theme for your WordPress website created now, with a visual builder, you can build whatever you want without even needing to know code.

Elementor Templates

The Elementor Template Library gives you access to hundreds of designer-made page layouts and blocks, all with premium high-end stock images, which you can use freely on your site.

As a small business, we assume that you want to dedicate as much time to your actual company as possible. This means efficiently building a great digital presence for your company, and then getting back to work. To help speed up the process of building any website, Elementor offers a template library of over 150 individual pages. Each page can be easily downloaded onto your website and gives you a great starting point when it comes to building your website.

Instead of building pages from scratch (which can be done easily in Elementor), you can download the page that best suits your need, and then edit it using the visual builder completely customizing it to your branding, content, and more.

In many templates, there will be placeholder images and placeholder content, that is easily replaced by images of your company, staff, and more. The placeholder content can easily be changed in the visual builder to match your company. For example, if you're changing in about page, there will be a placeholder section where you put your about content.

In addition to the templates provided by Elementor, there are tons of other sources like Envato Elements. With Elements, you get access to over 2,000 Elementor page templates spread across 70 template kits, including block templates and templates for Elementor Popup Builder.

Once you install and activate the free Envato Elements plugin, you'll be able to browse all the available templates from inside your WordPress dashboard and choose which ones to import.

For anybody looking to build a website quickly and easily, we always recommend using templates. Why reinvent the wheel? The template functionality in Elementor is a core feature, and because of this, you can build a website extremely quickly that is completely customized to your company.

Using templates allows you to save time. If you're a small business owner, you'll want to devote as much time as possible to your actual business, while still creating a stunning digital presence. Elementor, and its template library will allow you to do this. That's why we're going to be pushing the use of templates throughout this book. Even better, all of these templates are professionally designed, and will effectively convey the content that they contain. Sometimes, if you don't focus on design the content can get difficult to understand for visitors, hurting more than helping. Using professionally designed templates eliminates this risk.

However, if you want to build your pages from scratch, that's perfectly valid, and the principles outlined in this book will still apply to you.

Elementor Plugins & Community

By now, we've established that Elementor will allow you to build a completely custom website visually, eliminating the need for a web designer and advanced knowledge in coding. We've also discussed why using WordPress is a good idea, and why the Elementor template library will allow you to save immense quantities of time by using predesigned pages and customizing them to fit your business.

The final thing that should make Elementor so appealing to you is the robust community and third-party support around it.

There are thousands of plugins that are built to be compatible with Elementor. If you need any functionality, you will be able to find a plugin that is compatible with your Elementor. Additionally, there are plugins called add-on packs for Elementor that easily offer you new elements. These can seriously increase the design of your website and offer tons of more functionality. Will be discussing Elementor add-on packs at a further point in this book.

If you need any support, there's a robust Official Facebook Group of thousands of individuals who use Elementor. If you have any questions, posting in that Facebook group will typically result in a ton of answers regarding the platform. There are also many online support communities and forums dedicated to elementary simply due to the size and user base that Elementor has. If you need any support with your

website, feel free to join our community
ElementorQA.com.

Elementor Vs Others Platforms

We already discussed competing platforms with WordPress, but we wanted to compare industry leading platforms to WordPress and Elementor. Squarespace, Wix, and Weebly champion their user friendliness and simplicity as the major selling points of their products. The standard version of WordPress can be fairly complicated to understand, but when compared to these other page builders, WordPress offers a ton of additional functionality and features.

WordPress' competitors have one major advantage to the platform. They've focused on simplicity because there is a need in the market for an easy and simple way to build a website. You may be targeted by these companies as a small business, as you're looking for a very simple quick and easy way to build a completely custom website.

What Elementor does is bring simplicity to WordPress. You no longer need to know any code or hire a custom web developer to create a website for you when working with Elementor. This completely invalidates the need for any additional platforms. You really get the best of both worlds, you're able to build a website using WordPress, which is the world's most popular & powerful content management system. With WordPress, you can add whatever functionality you may think of. You also get immense simplicity when it comes to the actual building of your website, as the

Elementor page builder is drag-and-drop and doesn't require you to know any code.

You also save a lot on costs. Prices vary, but with the WordPress competition you'll be paying anywhere from $20 to $100 per month for a system that's fairly limited. What you're paying for is simplicity. When it comes to Elementor and WordPress, WordPress is free, and Elementor costs around $40 per year. Your only additional cost is hosting which ranges from $3 to $10 per month. You'll be able to cut your costs while accessing a super flexible and functional platform, without needing to know any code.

Page Builders

When it comes to WordPress, Elementor is not the only page builder offering out there. There are several competing page builders that eat into Elementor's market share.

As an agency, we've used every single page builder on the market in the past, and Elementor has remained on top as our favorite page builder for both us, and our clients. When we compare Elementor to other page builders like Divi, WordPress Bakery, and more, Elementor offers the perfect balance of simplicity with functionality. You can use Elementor to build whatever you want, and if you know advanced coding and functionality, you can incorporate that into your element or website. At the same time, everything is drag and drop and super simple and easy to understand, which means that the tool is perfect for those who are just looking for a powerful way to build a custom website.

When you compare Elementor to the other page builders, all alternative builders are lacking one of those two dimensions. Some page builders offer immense flexibility and power, like the ability to add PHP code directly into a page, build with CSS and more (Oxygen Builder) but they are difficult to understand for everyday users. Some page builders don't offer any functionality at all, and some page builders are simply difficult and outdated.

Elementor is the gold standard when it comes to simplicity paired with functionality, and is always our recommended page builder for every day consumers. It's also the most popular page builder for the reasons we've outlined above (5,000,000+ Installations), and the third-party support that comes with it is one of the best communities we've found online so far.

What You'll Need To Build This Site

We hope that the previous section properly introduced you to Elementor an WordPress. You should understand why using Elementor paired with WordPress is a great option when it comes to building a completely custom website for you or your small business. In this next section, we're going to go over the individual things that you'll need to create a website with WordPress in Elementor. You can use this section as a checklist of all the items that you'll need for your website.

Domain

Any website needs a domain. The domain is what you type into the browser search bar, hit enter, and end up on a website. Chances are, your business already has a domain. If you fall into that category, you can skip ahead to the next section in this evening. If you don't, let's talk about how best to acquire a domain.

Our agency uses a service called Namecheap to purchase domains. Namecheap is, as its name suggests, fairly cheap, and easy to use.

We always recommend that you **purchase a .com domain name.** You may be tempted to go ahead and get a domain name like ".art" if you are an artist, something a bit outdated like ".net" or something that isn't standard like ".studio".

Getting anything other than a .com domain name is statistically proven to push visitors away and make your business look less credible. We always recommend getting a .com domain name, even when other domain names may look more appealing, and be cheaper.

A .com domain will typically cost you around at $9 per year. We like Namecheap because it offers free identity protection. When you register a domain, you are required by law to give contact information. This information contains your email, name, address, and more. All of this information can easily be accessed via a database online (WhoIS Registry).

The free identity protection service replaces your information with the Namecheap's information and ensures that you don't have any domain related contact information out there.

Purchasing the domain is very simple. All you need to do is go to their website, enter your domain name into their search bar on the home page, see if it's available, and hit the buy button. The company will try to upsell you on various products, but all you need is a domain name from them at this point.

Your domain name is also directly associated with your email. In the industry, the best practice is to have a separate Mail hosting server, and web hosting server. This is so if one goes down, you can access your customer group with the other, and let them know of the problem.

Typically, if you're a small business, you don't have to many employees. This means that you can afford the $6 a month per user G Suite plan for email. With Namecheap, all you need to do is add G Suite to your cart, purchase it, and everything else will be set up automatically.

Once you've purchased your domain name and hosting, you can leave it be for now. We won't be connecting the domain name to your website until it's ready to go live, and your email should automatically be set up.

Hosting

One of the more important aspects of a WordPress website is the hosting. Your website is made up of files, and the files need to be stored on a server that can be accessed by the public. Whenever a visitor enters your domain name into their browser, the files that make up your website are requested from the public server, downloaded onto the browser, and shown to the visitor in the form of a website.

To be able to have a public website, you need a server to store your website files on.

For being such an important part of a WordPress website, hosting is also one of the most misrepresented services out there, with tons of misinformation going around. It's very easy to get locked into a three year contract with a bad webhost because you take recommendations from blogs who are paid to write about their respective service.

At the very base of the spectrum you have web hosting services that cost $1 to $5 per month. These plans are offered by companies like Bluehost, GoDaddy, and more. There called shared hosting plans and put many (dozens of) websites onto an individual server.

This is why they are able to offer plans at such a low price, because there are tons of websites on an individual server. Due to their low cost, high advertising spend, and hefty affiliate programs (as an agency I could make $65 per referral to many shared hosting provider), these plans dominate the market.

However, if you're serious about building a robust website for your business, **this is the worst choice possible when it comes to hosting**. Shared hosting means there are hundreds of websites on one server sharing the finite amount of CPU and memory processing power. When you have multiple websites sharing static resources, all of the websites are negatively impacted because they typically don't get the amount of processing power that they need.

This is especially true with modern WordPress and Elementor installations, as you'll need a lot of RAM (a lot is a relative term here) to run a website quickly and smoothly. Purchasing shared hosting will always come back to bite you, and you truly do get what you pay for.

It's also easy to get blinded by the unlimited storage, but most websites will only take up to five through 10 gigabytes at their largest. Unlimited storage shouldn't be a big selling point, and it's only a buzz word.

As a final thought on budget hosting, the typical contract duration to lock in the lowest price is 3 years. That means you need to pre pay for three years of budget hosting, and even with a one month money back guarantee, if your website outgrows its plan within the period you've paid for, there's no way to get any money back. It may be $2-7 per month, but you may end up spending $200-300 upfront to access those "monthly" prices.

By now, you should understand that you don't want to be paying for these budget hosting plans from Bluehost or other providers. At the same time, you don't want to be paying $200 per month for an enterprise level hosting plan that doesn't make any sense for your website.

To isolate exactly what we should be looking for in a hosting plan, we need to understand three basic principles. First, you want at least 1 GB of dedicated RAM for your installation. If you decide to do any E-Commerce on the website, then you want to allocate 2 GBs. The Elementor page builder specifies that you need at least 256 MB of RAM, but we found that giving it anywhere between 512 MB to 1 GB of RAM allows it to run at its optimal speed.

This means that on the back end, the page builder will load extremely quickly for you, so you won't be sitting in waiting for 20 seconds for the thing to load, and on the front end, your website will be delivered to its visitors extremely quickly.

As we said before, unlimited storage doesn't really matter. What does matter is the hardware that the website files are stored on. You need solid-state drives, typical hard drives with spinning disks are extremely slow, and will seriously impact the performance of your website.

Finally, if you are writing a blog and/or expect your site to grow in size and viewership in the future, you don't want be locked into any yearly contracts. Yearly contracts are inflexible in both pricing, and scalability. You want to be able to increase your server size, processing power, and memory at a moments notice, as your website traffic in size increases. You also want to be paying month per month, so you're not locked into any contracts.

Finally, hosting isn't just about a server. Purchasing hosting means you should be purchasing a managed service that offers security sweeps, free SSL certificates, automatic updates, and more. You don't want to be managing this all yourself, you want the hosting company to be doing this for you.

Our official agency recommendation is to use enterprise level cloud hosting for any website, large or small. Providers include Amazon Web Services, Google, Digital Ocean, and more and others that offer you the scalability that you need, the power that your website requires, and allows you to pay month by month. Also, due to the scale of cloud hosting providers, they can offer you a lot of resources at a very reasonable price. For example, for $5 a month, Digital Ocean will give you 1 GB of RAM, 25 GB of solid-state drive storage, and a lot more processing power. Note that this is almost the same pricing as shared hosting plans, except you're getting your own server with the resources that you need.

You can also choose to increase your plan at any time. So, if you require more storage, you can purchase another 25 gigabytes for $2 per month. If you need more ram, you can upgrade your entire plan to a 50 gigabyte solid state drive storage, 2 GB of RAM for $10 per month

The main drawback with enterprise level cloud hosting is that it's extremely complicated for a typical consumer, and bare bones. *There's no managed aspect to it*. So, if you were to perchance your own Digital Ocean server, you would need to run security sweeps yourself, update everything yourself, and understand the actual theory behind the host in order to set it up properly. As a small business owner, you don't want to be doing this, nor do you have time for it.

That's where managed cloud hosting services come in. These services offer cloud hosting through one of the five top cloud hosts, like AWS or Digital Ocean, and also manages the hosting for you. What this means is that they will run security sweeps on your cloud hosting server, automatically update WordPress, plugins, PHP versions in more, offer 24/7 live support, and more. This is exactly what you need.

Our agency recommends a service called Cloudways. They allow you to install WordPress on a Digital Ocean server in three clicks, and offer the managed aspect of hosting, with amazing 24/7 live support.

Their platform allows you to manage your WordPress installation, understand if you need to upgrade your server/computing power, install SSL certificates quickly, change domains, and more. In this book, and subsequent video tutorials, we will be using this host.

If you are creating a basic business website without any E-commerce, the cheapest plan that they offer is more than enough for you. The cheapest plan costs $10 per month, allows you to host your website on Digital Ocean servers, gives you 25 GB of solid state drive storage, and 1 GB of RAM. If you think back, we stated that Elementor recommends 256 MB, but hosting it on a server that offers something between 512 MB and 1 GB allows it to run extremely quickly. Our agency hosts all of our Elementor web sites on Cloudways, following the same memory allocations. It works well, the managed aspect is automatic, and the company bills you monthly.

As a small business owner, the support aspect of hosting is extremely important. You don't have an agency to email to ask any questions, so you need to rely on the hosting company. We've found that with Cloudways live support, you can ask them to do something, and they won't just point you into a documentation article, they'll do it for you.

(We'll be discussing the actual aspect of setting up Cloudways hosting at a later point in this book).

Elementor

Elementor is the core product that we will be using to build our website with WordPress. Elementor offers both a free and paid version. The free version is fairly limited and won't allow you to do many of the functionalities and features that we mentioned in this book. Elementor Pro costs $49.00 per year, and allows you to build a completely custom website. When you compare it to other solutions that allow you to do this, namely Squarespace, Elementor and WordPress are the more cost-effective options.

To build your website using Elementor and WordPress, you're going to need to purchase a license to Elementor Pro. This license gives you access to the support, features, and future updates for the plugin.

Plugins

There are a few additional plugins that we recommend installing onto your WordPress website. We're going to mention each plug-in here briefly, and then revisit the plug-in when discussing building your actual website. Each plug-in that we mentioned here fulfills a specific task for your WordPress website, and is essential to the success and viability of it.

First, we're going to discuss the individual plugins here, and then discuss installing and configuring them at a later point in this book. This section is meant to just give you a basic checklist of all the things that you're going to need to get to create your WordPress website.

Free plugins can easily be installed via the WordPress repository, which we will discuss later in this book. Paid plugins will need to be installed by downloading the plugin files from their developer, uploading them to your WordPress website, installing the individual plugin, and then connecting the license key. We will also discuss this process at a later point in this book.

The first essential plugin for your WordPress website is one that deals with security.

WordFence

The top WordPress security plugin is also free and called WordFence. WordFence offers a web application firewall (WAF), which will block hackers from accessing your website. IP addresses known to be associated with hackers will automatically be blocked from your website.

Hackers who attempt to run brute force attacks on your website will be blacklisted, and removed from being able to access your website as well. WordFence is automatically installed and configured, which means you don't need much technical know how to properly secure your WordPress website.

Envato Elements

Elementor comes with a hefty collection of templates, but we prefer using templates from a third party provider called Envato Elements. This plugin offers you 100+ template kits, and over 2000 individual pages for free.

SendInBlue STMP

When a user submits a contact form on your website, you should be receiving an email that a contact form has just been submitted. To send that email, you need a service that will do that. We recommend using a service called SendInBlue STMP, which will automatically enable outbound emails from your WordPress website. Both the plugin and the service are free. SendInBlue allows your WordPress website to send up to 200 emails per day for free.

Breeze

This is a free plugin that increases the performance and speed of your website. Having a website that loads quickly is absolutely essential to the success of it. If your website loads in more than 3 seconds, 50% of your visitors will click away from it, Google will rank it lower than a faster website, and users that end up on the website will have a poor experience. Breeze will automatically optimize all files on your website too be served to your visitors quickly, resulting in a very low page speed time.

It's important to note that this plugin only works properly with Cloudways hosting. If you're not using Cloudways hosting for your website, you want to look into a performance plugin, but one that's not Breeze (we like WPRocket).

Rank Math

Rank Math is a free search engine optimization plugin that will tell you how readable your individual pages and posts are by Google. It will also help you optimize all content on your website to ensure maximum visibility from search engines. This is a free plug-in, that is extremely powerful and works well with Elementor.

These are the essential plugins that our agency recommends you install on your website, but there are several additional plugins that will be mentioned throughout this book. The additional plugins mentioned throughout this book are optional but may add individual functionality to your website. Additionally, you may opt to add additional plugins not mentioned in this book that suit the needs of your company as well.

What Your Costs Will Be

Now, let's talk about the costs of your website.

The Elementor Pro plugin is going to be the most expensive purchase when it comes to creating your website. Elementor Pro currently costs $49.00 per year.

Your domain will cost $9 per year to maintain, (depending on the provider that you use this cost may vary). Sometimes, you can get a domain for free, or at a discounted price.

The hosting for your website will cost $10 per month. This is billed month to month.

That means that your **average monthly cost will be around $15, all inclusive**. Let's compare these costs to competing services like Squarespace & Wix. When comparing these costs, we're going to choose the plans from the respective companies that best match the features and functionality offered by a WordPress website with Elementor.

Squarespace Commerce	Wix Pro
$26/month	$22/month

The Three Pillars Of Any Site

Before we begin discussing how to build your actual website, we want to review the three pillars that every website should follow. Whenever our agency begins a website design project, we take a look at these three individual pillars when creating the list of assets, plugins, code, and more that we will use to build the site. If you build the site around these three pillars, you'll end up with a great final product that will not only look good, but perform well, and offer value to your visitor.

Design

The first thing that you want to focus on is design. When it comes to website design, your website shouldn't just look good, but it should function well. That means that content should be laid out in a manner that is easily readable by your user, button links should go to where they say they'll go, descriptions should be descriptive, and the website should *just look good*. A well-designed website is more credible to a visitor, so focusing on design is an absolutely essential part of creating any website.

If you opt to use templates, you'll have a head start when it comes to design, as these templates are created by professional designers.

We always recommend using a template, or at least getting inspiration from existing projects when it comes to design. There are several web sites that we, as an agency, use to get design for new projects.

- Awwwards.com
- Siteinspire.com

You can use these resources to identify web sites in your industry, and then mirror the structure of the individual pages. All of your pages should be easy to navigate, understand, and read. These three points – navigation, readability, and easy of use -- are what separates a well-designed website from a poorly designed website.

Also, keep in mind that when it comes to design, sometimes simplicity is better. A simple, well designed website will always be a better option than a website with tons of individual elements popping out at the user in every which way.

Think about the best example when it comes to simplicity: Apple. All of Apple's products are super simple and easy to use, while incorporating good design. This potent combination is what makes Apple the most valuable company in the world.

Branding & Consistency

If you are a small business that's developing and designing your own website, we recommend working off the design styling of your logo. A typical logo will contain colors, typography, and design styling that can be used throughout your website. This is a great starting point, especially if you're not working with a professional designer when it comes to creating your website.

Having a consistent design style throughout your website makes your digital presence professional. That means that you should use the same font for the entire website (pairing fonts is a good idea, where you have an individual font for headers and headings, and you have an individual font for body text). You should also use the same color scheme throughout the website.

Typically, you'll have a primary color, a secondary color, an accent color, and a body color. You can also have a color specifically for your text. The primary color will be your main brand color and typically is applied to all headings. The secondary color is used as, you guested, a secondary backup color to the primary color. The accent color is used for links and buttons, while the body color is used for the background.

The layout, and styling of each individual page will definitely change depending on the content contained, but it should follow the same standard design language. For example, if you're using rounded borders on individual buttons on one page, you should be using rounded borders on individual buttons on another page.

You can use a tool to generate professional color schemes from your base branding colors like Coolors.co.

Do you need to layout pages?
At our agency, every project starts out with mockups, and wireframes of individual pages. If you're creating a

simple business website that only contains 4 or 5 pages, you may not need to do this. Instead, you can design the pages as you build them, which will save you time and resources.

Again, we recommend using templates to create your individual pages, and then taking the placeholder content in those templates and replacing it with your own. However, if you're looking to design your own individual pages, or have a website with more than four or five pages, you may want to at least sketch out the individual pages of your website so you can understand the styling, design, structure, of the website.

When it comes to the design of your website, you should focus on simplicity, consistency, and ease of use. These individual elements culminate in a well designed user experience that will generate more leads, a higher conversion rate, and look more professional. Using templates, or getting inspiration from existing professionally designed websites will help you in this regard, and we highly recommend doing that.

Security

We touched upon the importance of website security when discussing WordFence, the main plugin that we use on all of our websites for security, but this is an absolutely essential part of any website design project, and you should create your website with security at the forefront.

First, let's go over why you should actually secure your WordPress website.

First and foremost, if your visitor ends up on your web page, and is immediately bombarded with pop-up ads and redirects, they will click away. Your business will lose revenue, as well as credibility. This is the most typical and least serious thing that a website hack will result in.

If the hack escalates to a more serious level, the hacker can steal your user information. This means customer emails and contact information can be captured from the website. In a worst-case scenario, the hacker can log entries into the website, and gather credit card numbers and other sensitive data if you had payment processing on your site.

If you are processing sensitive customer information, then you can be legally liable if your website gets hacked.

People have realized how serious consumer data privacy and security is, which is why we're seeing a lot of regulation in this area. For example, if you serve customers in the EU, the GDPR applies to you. GDPR is a regulation that requires businesses to protect the personal data and privacy of EU citizens for transactions that occur within EU member states. In the US there federal laws as well as state specific laws for data privacy. If you're interested in the legalities surrounding website security, go check out this impressive curated list of every law in the United States that could apply to your
website: https://www.csoonline.com/article/2126072/c

ompliance-the-security-laws-regulations-and-guidelines-directory.html

If you have secured your website, you can build consumer trust by showing the measures you've taken to protect their information. You can do this through a blogpost, through a dedicated security page, or through footer badges. Did you know that choosing the right badge / seal can actually increase your conversion rate?

65% of online shoppers felt that the Norton™ Secured Seal was reassurance that the site would not give them a virus and was safe to browse.

Of course, to get this badge, you need a secure website to start off with.

Addressing security concerns will make your website's conversion rate higher, your company more incredible, and reduce the risk of any bad actors causing problems for your digital presence.

Performance

In 2020, having a fast website is incredibly important. Google incorporates website speed and performance into their ranking algorithm, so a faster website will rank higher and their search engine. Additionally, if your website takes over 3 seconds to load, 50% of your visitors will click away from it.

There's no point to creating a website that slow to load, as you'll be missing out on visitors, and this may impact your credibility. For example, as a consumer, would you be comfortable putting your trust in a website that takes over 10 seconds to load?

Creating a fast website begins during the build process. You need to create your individual pages with performance in mind.

The more elements (headings, links, sections, paragraphs...) you have on your page, the slower the page can get. Breaking up large pages into multiple pages reduces the numbers of elements present, and makes the pages load quicker. For example, you can move the "Services" section from the homepage and make it into its own page. On the homepage, you can add links and short services descriptions.

Make sure you design your pages to be lean, and quick.

After you're done building your individual website pages, running a complete optimization of your website is needed. We recommended a plugin called Breeze in our recommended plugin section of this book. Breeze will automatically compress files to be smaller, add a caching system in place on the website, and offer additional performance capabilities.

If you have an image heavy website, you may want to focus on optimizing images which includes resizing them to be optimal sizes for your website, compressing them, and serving them in next Gen formats. We recommend using a plugin called Imagify which will do this automatically.

If you're interested in creating a super fast and high performing website, check out our blog at isotropic.co/blog.

Also, if you don't want to optimize your website for performance yourself because it's too complicated, consider our service at SpeedOpp.com, professional WordPress speed optimization.

The Structure Of A Corporate Website

Now that you understand the three pillars of any website, let's begin thinking about how to structure your individual corporate website.

Think Like A Visitor

When you first begin thinking about the individual pages and structure of your website, you should think like a visitor. What would your visitor want to see when they enter your website? Thinking like a visitor allows you to properly offer the necessary information that visitors actually want to see. The whole point of a website is to offer a collection of information online that makes the visitors life easier, builds credibility, and ultimately leads to lead generation or conversion.

This book is going to recommend a standard set of pages, but depending on your business, you may have other needs. We recommend running customer research before building your website, so you can best understand what content you should be offering. This customer research can be as simple as asking somebody who walks into your store, what would you like to see on a website for our company? You can also email existing customers a survey, or conduct market research using a paid route.

Whatever the case is, you should fully understand what your visitors are expecting from a website before building it. There's no point to creating a website if it isn't suiting the needs of your visitors, as your visitors are going to be your customers. A website isn't created for you, it is created to further your business, and to further your business you need to meet the needs and requirements of your visitors.

Essential Pages

Now that we understand what needs to go in to determine the structure of your website, let's talk about the essential pages of every corporate website. Keep in mind, that this page collection is tailored for a small local business and may change depending on the needs of your visitors.

You should include pages that offer valuable information to your visitors and build your company's credibility. You should not include pages to stuff your website with content. Only include the necessary pages that you know that your visitors will want. We find that creating pages that are not necessary to your company lead to lower conversion rates. You may think that including as many pages as possible is good for SEO, but this is the opposite. For SEO, you should focus on providing valuable content in the form of blog posts, rather than tons of pages that visitors don't actually need or visit.

First, before discussing the individual pages, let's discuss the actual structure of the website. Your website should be online for 2 major reasons. The 1st reason is building credibility. You build credibility with good content that tells the visitor what you're about and good design. The second reason should be conversion and lead generation. And this is where the structure of the website comes in to play. You want your website to make a visitor who is interested about your services convert into a customer. The way you do this is by presenting relevant information, building credibility, and funneling the visitor to a contact form or a checkout page. That means that the actual structure of the website should be funneling your visitor to whatever your final conversion may be.

We assume that most of our readers are small business owners, which means that you want to be funneling your visitors to the contact page, so they send a contact form requesting more information. This is known as a lead, and you want your website to generate as many leads as possible.

The way to generate as many leads as possible is to build your website in a funnel shape. The homepage collects all your visitors, points them to what they're looking for, and then from the content that they are reading, they're funneled to the contact form. So, an example flow through the website would be home page, to services page, to contact page.

You need to build your website to make your conversion pages visible as possible. If your conversion page is the contact page, and your conversion is a contact form submission, you need to add many call to actions and buttons to the contact page. For example, under the services page, having a call to action that says contact us now to learn more about this individual service will make you're lead generation form easily accessible to the visitor.

Whenever you're building a website you need to focus on credibility, and conversion. The structure of the website is absolutely important to the conversion and should always be built in a funnel towards your conversion device. For small businesses, conversion devices are typically contact forms, so you need to make the contact form comment in the page that they're contained on as visible and easy to access as possible.

As an agency, for the majority of our websites, they'll be containing these following pages:

Home

The home page is the main landing page of your website, and should be designed to point your visitors in the direction of essential content. The home page should contain short blurbs of content that you know your visitors are looking for. For example, you should contain a phone number, email address, about blurb, and more in the initial viewport. You should contain links to your individual services, links to your about page, and additional content that you know that your visitors are looking for.

At the same time, you shouldn't overload your home page with content. Tons of text on a home page leads to lower conversion rates and a higher bounce rate (visitors only will end up on one page, and then navigate away from your website), because loads of small words on one page is not user friendly unless the visitor is looking for specific information that requires a large word count.

Instead of putting all your content on one individual page and making it the homepage, you should make the homepage point to additional pages that offer category specific information.

About

The about page provides valuable information to your visitor regarding your company. The about page should accurately present the values, people, and service that your company provides. It's meant to build credibility with your visitor, and get them understanding what you guys are about.

Additional sub pages can include a staff page, a history page, and more. For example, if your company has been around since the 1800s, including a history page will definitely increase the credibility of your company. If you have a robust collection of staff who are highly educated and experienced in your field, including a staff page complete with staff biographies will build the credibility of your company and showcase why your visitors should work with you as opposed to a competitor.

Services

If your company offers services to any customer group, be it business to business or business to consumer, you should offer a page that discusses the services that you offer. This page should accurately identify all the services you offer and may also include testimonials and other credibility building devices.

Blog

Publishing a well written blog serves as a two-pronged approach to marketing. First, visitors who are already on your website will see that you have a well written, knowledgeable blog which establishes you as a thought leader in your field. This content builds credibility with the visitor, and will increase conversions because they trust that you know what you're actually talking about.

A blog also generates traffic for your website which can result in targeted conversions. If you publish a blog consistently, and make sure your website is optimized for maximum search engine visibility, you will generate a lot of inbound traffic, and the inbound traffic will then convert into leads. We always recommend including a blog on your website and consistently publishing to it at least three to four times per month for visibility in search engines

The blog consists of the main archive page, where visitors are shown all of the blog posts published, and an individual blog post page.

Contact

The contact page offers essential contact information -- maybe a Google map of your location, a phone number, an email, **and a contact form**. This is where your visitor will convert into a lead, so this makes it one of the most important pages on the website. As we stated before, the website should be built to funnel your visitors into your conversion device. For most small businesses, the conversion device on a website is a contact form where visitors reach out for more information, and you can begin your offline sales process.

Your individual contact form is important, and there are tons of minute things that you should focus on when creating it. First off, the design and structure of the actual form impact conversion rates. Properly educating yourself in contact form design will ultimately lead to more leads. This is a good investment of your time period there are tons of free resources online that you can read about contact forms, and we always recommend using HubSpot education when it comes to design that impact sales and lead generation. here, we're going to list a couple of blog posts that we find helpful in our agency:

https://blog.hubspot.com/marketing/form-design

This blog post discuss is the best practices of contact form design in great detail period understanding these best practices will help you create a contact form that has higher conversions.

The essential takeaways from the best practices of a contact form are as follows. Creating a simple to understand contact form that is one column leads to the best conversion rate. Arranging the form fields from easiest to hardest will also lead to a very high conversion rate. For example, a very easy field to fill out would be a name field. A medium difficulty field would be the email field. And a hard field to fill out would be the message field.

There are a bunch of additional best practices that you should focus on when it comes to contact form design, which is why you should educate yourself on how best to create this aspect of your website. Luckily, with Elementor, you can build a contact form to match any design or styling you need, which we will be discussing at a later point in this book.

https://blog.hubspot.com/service/best-contact-us-pages

As we've mentioned multiple times throughout this book, using existing, well designed websites and elements as inspiration is a good idea, especially if you're not a professional designer. This blog post shows you 30 contact pages that are very well designed, and you can incorporate these designs into your own website.

All too many times, businesses will simply slap a contact form on the contact page and call it a day. This is not what should be done because the contact page is the most important aspect of the website. If you're looking to generate leads, the leads will be generated on this page, and a well designed contact form is essential to building credibility and increasing your conversion rate.

Luckily, using a template provided by Elementor or Envato will help you create a well designed contact page. Elementor also has an integrated form builder, with spam protection, which we will be discussing at a later point in this book.

Other Structural Things

There are a couple other structural aspects and elements that we should discuss when it comes to building your website. First, called the actions are extremely powerful and simple devices that will lead to more lead generation. Creating a proper call to action and placing it in a good spot is something that you should focus on.

In simplest terms, your call to action will direct a user to do something. For a small business, a typical call to action would be placed on a page or a blog post, and would direct visitors to the contact form. The call to action would be "contact us for more information".

Properly placing call to actions throughout the website that direct your visitors to the conversion device, which in most cases is the contact page, will lead to increased conversions.

As always, taking a look at existing call to actions that are proven to work is a good idea when designing your own. This blog post identifies a couple caller actions that work well, and you can copy the design off these.

https://blog.hubspot.com/marketing/call-to-action-examples

Like contact forms, there are series of best practices for call to actions. There are also tons of studies that identify principles that you can use when it comes to creating call to actions. These studies go as far as identifying the best millimeter spacing between buttons and texts, contrast ratios, and more. If you want to get involved in that aspect of building call to actions, feel free.

https://www.wordstream.com/blog/ws/2014/10/09/call-to-action

However, we recommend you simply focus on three main rules when it comes to building call to actions, and have had success from following them.

1. A no-obligation statement

2. Some updated version of "mail your acceptance card"

3. sense of urgency around responding right away.

Creating a no obligation statement like "contact us for more information", or "Join Now for free" is essential to a high click rate on the call to action. In your case, having your call to action point to a contact form, and identifying that this contact is free is a good idea.

"Mail your acceptance card" was the typical call to action that was found in magazines and print publications before the Internet. Adopting this proven, Age old technique to fit your digital call to action, is a good idea. in most cases, stating fill out this quick contact form to learn more is very similar to the Mail your acceptance card message.

For increased conversion rates, creating a sense of urgency around your call to action is a good idea. If you're a service business, you can offer a discount that expires on a certain date. If your visitor contacts you before that certain date, they will get the discount, and if they don't they won't get the discount. This encourages a higher conversion rate because there is an incentive behind clicking on the button and filling out the form.

Finally, properly structuring your pages is also a good idea. If you're using templates, you don't really need to worry about this as the pages are typically created by professional designers. However, keeping in mind that a website is very similar to a book, and should be let read from left to right is a good idea. Headers should be bold, and easy to read. Content should go from left to right. Pages should be structured in a simple and easy to understand manner.

SEO

When it comes to building a website, talking about search engine optimization is a necessary evil. This section is going to discuss search engine optimization in its most basic form, but SEO is extremely complex an ever changing.

https://ahrefs.com/blog/seo-basics

This is a great resource for people looking to get started in SEO. Because this book isn't about SEO, we're not going to dive into great detail, but instead you should rely on high quality blogs and knowledge bases to learn this yourself.

The most basic principles of SEO are offering your customers high quality, keyword optimized articles consistently. That's why we push including a blog on your business website in this book. Having a blog allows you to publish high quality content consistently, which will lead to more inbound traffic, and more conversions to leads.

You will want to learn about keyword optimization, and general WordPress search engine optimization. We will be introducing and SEO plug in at a later point in this book that will automate most of the optimization for you when it comes to pages and posts.

A great way to learn about SEO is reading the blog for this plugin, which can be found at:

https://rankmath.com/blog/

while the content changes, the general premise of the blog is "beginner education in search engine optimization". They offer actionable techniques that you can use to make your website rank higher on Google.

We will say that the major players in the SEO industry will overcharge you by a massive margin for their services. Most SEO can easily be done after learning essential techniques online. If you are a local small business, in no scenario does it make any sense to be paying $900 a month for somebody to write you blog articles optimized for keywords.

In many cases, it's a good idea to offload digital services, which removes the need to learn about them. In this case, educating yourself on what SEO truly is, and how it works is a good investment of your time. In a few hours you will be able to optimize your website yourself, or at least be knowledgeable in the topic when speaking to an SEO professional and not get scamed.

Two additional things that you should consider when thinking about search engine optimization is website usability and website performance. You need to ensure that your website loads quickly , as a slow loading website is penalized in Google search engine rankings. You also need to make sure that your website is well designed and user-friendly, as Google has several mechanisms that will allow it to identify a website that isn't user friendly. If your site is difficult to use, for example if buttons are too small, if links are broken, if contrast ratios are off, then Google will penalize it in its rankings.

Properly educating yourself in this arena will pay off when your website garners a lot of traffic, and begins generating leads on autopilot because of it.

Be on the lookout for another ebook in the next couple of months from Isotropic regarding small business search engine optimization that you can do yourself.

(Join the Ebook Mailing list for launch notifications and giveaways: https://isodes.link/ebook-email-list)

Building Your WordPress Website With Elementor

By now, we've reviewed the essential components of a WordPress website, what Elementor is, and what you should keep in mind when building and designing your website. Now, let's discuss the actual process of creating an Elementor website from start to finish. In this section we're going to discuss the installation of WordPress, setting up development environments, setting up individual plugins, and creating basic pages with Elementor. By the end of this section, you should be comfortable creating a basic website with Elementor. We're also going to link you to several resources that will help you answer any questions you may have.

Using A Development Environment

There are a bunch of reasons that you would want to build locally, or not on your final webhost. First, you can save several months of payments for production hosting, as you won't need to be paying for your life server when developing.

You may also just want to play around with WordPress and test it out, and it wouldn't make any sense purchasing traditional web hosting, which is oriented towards those who are trying to bring a website live and offer it to the public.

Developing also involves adding, removing, and testing multiple plug-ins, themes, and database configurations. All of this will add bloat to your server, so you definitely want to do this on an environment created for development, and then move your website to a live server.

There are very few drawbacks when it comes to developing your website on a different hosting infrastructure then your production host. The only additional step that doing this requires is migrating the development website to the live web host, which is a really simple and easy thing to do.

Now that we understand why you probably want to be developing a website on a separate platform, let's go over 4 options that you have. As an agency, we've used every single one of these options and each has its own pros and cons.

WAMP

WampServer is software that basically allows you to install a fully functional web hosting framework on to your computer. This means you can locally host, develop, and edit WordPress (as well as other web).

WAMP is an acronym that stands for Windows, Apache, MySQL, and PHP. It's a software stack which means installing WAMP installs Apache, MySQL, and PHP on your operating system (Windows in the case of WAMP).

If you've been involved in setting up hosting installations, you may have heard of LAMP. LAMP is a collection of software that allows you to run WordPress on Linux.

If you're installing WordPress into any generic web host, you're probably using a LAMP stack (collection of software that allows you to run WordPress). WAMP does the same thing just on your own computer.

We really like using this to mess around with ideas of ours, because it allows us to really quickly and easily access the files behind WordPress. This means we can drag-and-drop plugins, themes, and quickly edit files on our native text editor in Windows.

There's no need for FTP, or SSH access because all of the files are stored locally on the computer.

Installing this to your computer is pretty simple, all you need to do is download and installation package, and it will automatically install a bunch of individual packages, and management software to your computer.

Then all you need to do is install WordPress, and begin developing. You develop your website on a localhost. What is means is instead of typing a domain name or IP address into your browser address bar, all you need to do is type localhost and the name of your installation. (ex. localhost/wpinstall).

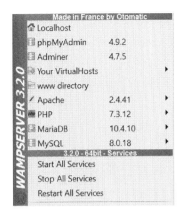

WordPress is then installed, and you can edit and code as you would on any traditional web hosting installation.

This is very powerful, and will allow you to tweak individual PHP settings, server settings, and more. It's great for developers, but simple enough for first-time users to figure out.

Keep in mind that you will definitely need to follow some tutorials to properly install the software, but once it's on the computer, and once you understand how to use it, it's super fast, powerful, and free.

Also, because you're hosting everything on your own computer, you can develop your website without an internet connection. On the flip side, you can't share your website (by sharing the link) with anybody on the internet without having to install additional software.

If you develop a website on WAMPserver, and then need to move it to a live web host, this is very simple. Just follow our guide here:

Local

If WAMP seems a bit technical for you (I don't blame you) then a simpler solution would be Local by Flywheel. This is also free, and allows you to host your website on your own computer.

Local is a much simpler version of WAMP, but if all you want to do is have a Sandbox where you can mess around with WordPress installations, this is the software for you.

SPEED AND SIMPLICITY
Flywheel is fast and functional, so we brought those features to the slickest local WordPress development application in the world.

SIMPLE DEMO URLS
Show off your latest work! Create shareable URLs to demo your local WordPress sites to clients, collaborators, friends, or adoring fans.

SSH + WP-CLI ACCESS
Local offers simple root SSH access to individual sites, so you can tinker around if your heart desires.

There are two things that we like about this service. The first thing is that it allows you to install WordPress in one click, and automatically sets up your database. This is very quick and simple, and compared to WAMP where you need to make your own database, it's much easier.

Local also allows you to create demo URLs, and share your website online, even though it's being locally-developed, This is a great feature to have, and though you shouldn't use it to access and develop your website online, it's perfect for sharing.

One drawback we have noticed is that Local is fairly slow.

Pushing changes, loading new changes, and more happened very slowly. We've tested this on multiple machines, but haven't seriously debug the issue as we typically use wamp. This is just something to keep in mind if you are going to use this service.

If you're looking for a super simple, minimal development environment for your computer, you should definitely check the service out. It's free!

Pantheon

Pantheon is an online WordPress host that is very oriented towards developers and Enterprise applications. They allow you to create up to 20 individual sandbox websites. When we build small to medium-sized WordPress websites, this is the service that we use, as it offers a lot for free.

Because this WordPress dev installation is hosted online, you can develop from anywhere, and share the link to other devs and clients.

This is a service created specifically for developers, so on the backend you can access a lot of powerful features as well. If you are in the Pantheon ecosystem, then you can easily move your website to a live hosting solution offered by them in one click, but we choose to use the development hosting on Pantheon, and then migrate the site to Cloudways or a dedicated Cloud host.

There's also a lot of Team specific features, which is great if you are a multi employee design and development agency. Everybody can work together pretty easily with this platform.

If you're doing a completely local installation for development, it's very difficult to have other people work on your project. That's more suited towards individuals, or somebody who's just looking to play around and test themes and features by themselves.

A drawback is that because it's hosted online, you'll need to connect via SFTP to access your WordPress files. At times, this solution can be somewhat slow as it lacks a lot of power. In those situations, we'll use the next option to develop.

Cloudways
When we're working on a large website, performance and speed is paramount to the success of the project. Sometimes, developing websites on infrastructure that won't be the same as the final platform doesn't make sense. That's because the website could be very heavy – slow to migrate with lots of big static files.

Getting a Speed and Performance right is necessary, so it doesn't make any sense to develop it on another platform, optimize it to run quickly on that platform, migrate, and then have to re optimize it to run quickly on a new platform.

For most of our large projects, we will use a dedicated Cloudways DigitalOcean installation. Cloudways is our host of choice, and most of our final project end up being hosted by them. This is because of their unique offering, which allows us to put the website on enterprise-level cloud hosting, and manage them quickly and easily. Adding new installations of WordPress takes three clicks.

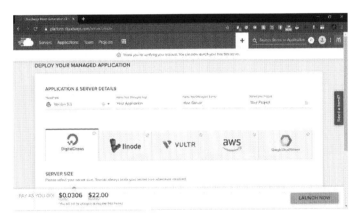

We will partition a new DigitalOcean installation to develop the website on, notisave cost we won't afford the project as many resources as it will get when it goes live. What this means in plain English is that we purchase hosting that has less RAM, storage, and CPU processing power than the final project.

This means we keep the monthly hosting costs down until we need to serve the website to the public, but can develop on the same platform that the website will be going live on. We can correctly configure all caching solutions, CDN, and more by going this route.

Like Pantheon, Cloudways offers a lot of team collaboration tools, so multiple designers and developers can work on the project at once.

When it's time to bring the website live, we will do one of two things. First, we'll check to see if the server is bloated from our development process. If the server is bloated, we will make a new server on Cloudways and migrate the website to the new server.

If the server isn't bloated, which is the typical scenario, will simply increase the processing power and storage to an optimal resource level for our end product. For example, we may develop using a $10 month DigitalOcean plan (through Cloudways), but then upscale the server to a $50 a month plan that has a lot more memory and Storage.

With the service, it's super simple to do: it takes three clicks and the server is upgraded automatically. All hosting, caching, domain configurations, SSL, DNS, and more remains the same.

Depending on the complexity of your website, and your desire to migrate, we recommend either using local, or Cloudways. For this example website that we will be discussing in this book, we're going to use the Local application to develop our website on our computer, and then migrate the website to a live Cloudways hosting environment.

Using Local

Local is designed to be super easy and user friendly. Even if you're not well versed in WordPress website development, installing, configuring, and using local is a very simple and easy thing to do. The first thing you need to do is download local onto your computer. You can do this by going on Google searching for Local by Flywheel, and then downloading and installing it as you would with any other application.

When you're installing Local, it will install other dependent libraries and applications on your computer. What local basically does is set up a collection of software packages that enables you to virtually host a website from your individual computer.

Once you've installed Local you can quickly and easily create a new WordPress installation. This base WordPress installation will be what we build our website with Elementor on. Once our website is done being developed on the local environment, will simply move it over to the live host, connect the domain, and your business will have a new website.

To create the actual installation, all you need to do is click the big plus button in the bottom left hand corner, and follow the setup wizard. The setup wizard will then walk you through naming the website, and collect a couple of details that will enable the application to automatically provision an installation of WordPress.

There are several advanced configuration options, but you can leave everything in its default form and end up with a perfectly functional version of WordPress that will work well.

The one thing you should change is the default email in the setup WordPress step. Change the default email which is dev.localbyfly…. to whatever Email address you use for business notifications. We recommend using your info@ email address as this is where the website will send all notifications. Once we install plugins on our website, we will be receiving notifications every time a user submits a form, or our security plugin detects an issue.

Local has a lot of powerful features that we'll be discussing at a later point in this book, but let's review a couple main functionalities now.

The first thing is that you can easily toggle a website on and off. When the website is on, you can access it and develop it locally from your individual computer. Because it is an installation on your computer, you can develop WordPress even if you don't have a connection to the Internet.

If you would like to share your website for feedback, this is easy to do. Local will allow you to create a temporary domain that you can share your website with. Like we said previously, this application basically allows you to host your website from your computer, and creating the temporary domain allows you to share your website to anybody on the Internet. You can toggle the domain on and off as you need it.

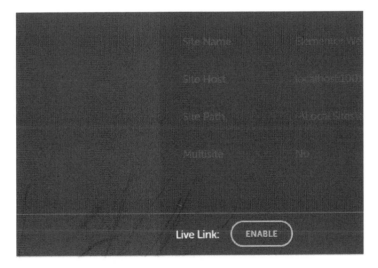

If you need to access advanced features such as the database, or set up mailing from a dev environment, this is very simple and easy to do with Local. there are several included functionalities that will allow you to do pretty much anything necessary to creating a well-functioning WordPress website on your computer.

You don't need to learn much more about Local than what we introduce here, but if you're interested in learning how to access and use the advanced features that it offers, feel free to check out these individual blog posts and knowledge base articles.

https://getflywheel.com/layout/local-by-flywheel/

The company that has developed local is called flywheel, and the above blog post is its introduction to the product.

If you need a super in depth article on how to get started with Local, check this post out:

https://getflywheel.com/layout/local-wordpress-development-environment-how-to/

In our case, there are only a few things that you really need to do. we've already discussed them above, but let's restate them now:

- download and install the local application
- click the add a new website button
- enter all the necessary information in the wizard, you don't need to change any advanced features (use the preferred environment)
- this tool will automatically provision an installation of WordPress on your local computer

Setting Up WordPress

Now that we've gone ahead and installed WordPress onto our computer, it's time to access it and set up the base installation. In this section, we're going to prepare the content management system and make sure everything is functioning before installing Elementor and building our website.

The first thing to do is access the WordPress installation. First, make sure that the website is active and running in Local.

In this example, you can see that the Elementor website is live because the status icon is green. The "SpeedOpp Clients" website is not live because the status icon is Gray.

Now, you can access the administrative back-end of your website by clicking on the "admin" button on the right hand side of your screen.

Clicking on this will load the default browser of your computer, and re direct you to the WordPress login screen of your new installation. This will be the WordPress installation that you build your Elementor website on period to access it, simply enter the username and password that you set in the setup stage with local.

Now, you'll find yourself on a factory fresh installation of WordPress. Here, we're going to run several checks to make sure WordPress is completely functional and ready for a website to be built on top of it.

The first thing we do is access the general tab of the settings screen. You can find this on the admin menu on the left hand side of your WordPress backend interface.

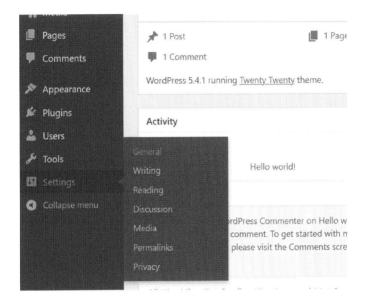

In this screen, we will verify the site title, site tag line, and administrative email address.

Then, we will access the front end of the website by navigating to the root domain of the installation. The base WordPress theme should be installed an completely functional. You can check that the theme is completely functional by clicking on several links and making sure they lead you to working pages.

As long as everything is functioning on the front end, and all the information is valid on the back end, you're now ready to begin the installation process of plugins and themes to your WordPress website.

Installing Themes

The first thing we're going to do on our clean installation of WordPress (after we have verified that everything is working well) is install a free theme called "Hello Elementor". To install a new theme, navigate to appearance, themes, and on the themes page click the add new button in the upper left hand corner.

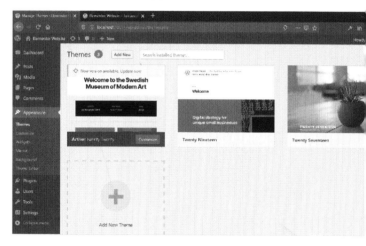

Then, search for Hello Elementor. Hover over the individual entry for that theme, and click on the install button.

Hello

Theme

I am text block. Click edit button to change this text. Lorem ipsum dolor sit amet, consectetur adipiscing elit. Ut elit tellus, luctus nec ullamcorper mattis, pulvinar dapibus leo.

Launch Project →

Lorem Ipsum is simply dummy text of the printing

There are many variations of passages of Lorem Ipsum

Where does it come from? Contrary to popular belief

Here are many variations of passages of Lorem Ipsum

Once the theme is installed, that same button will change to say "activate" click on the activate button, and the theme will be successfully installed on your website period to verify the installation, simply navigate to the front end of the website and your screen should look something like this:

This theme removes virtually all styling and structural components from your WordPress website. It gives you a blank canvas that you can easily install templates and build your website on top of. If you choose to use other themes (the Elementor builder *will* work with other themes) there may be compatibility issues due to other frameworks and coding on the themes end.

Installing Hello Elementor removes all possibilities of configuration and compatibility issues. Additionally, most templates that can be installed onto your Elementor website are designed to work with the Hello Elementor theme only because of the lack of compatibility issues.

Link Colors

Before we continue to any further step, we like setting the color of our links. While you can technically do this at any point throughout the process, setting the color of your links is something that we choose to do at this point because it is simple and easy.

From the front end of your website, you should see a customize button in the top bar of your WordPress website. Clicking on the customize button will load a user interface for your website. It should look something like this:

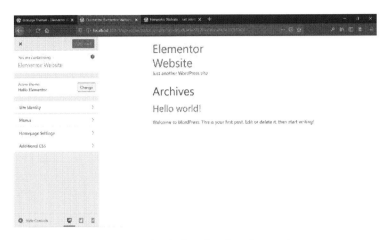

We're going to change the link color for the entire website by using basic CSS. Don't worry, we're going to give you the codes that you can easily copy and paste into your website if you don't understand CSS. We're also going to explain the meaning of every aspect of every snippet of code that we discuss in this book.

To change the links, click on the final tab which is titled "additional CSS" in the left hand menu.

In the text entry box, paste this code in:

a {color:#YOURCOLORHEXCODE;}

Here's what this code does. The "a" In the front identifies that the CSS code will impact all links on the website. In CSS, "a" represents a hyperlink. The bracket signifies that there is going to be code that is applied to that element "{}". inside the brackets, "color:" will change the text color of whatever element we are applying this to. In this case, we're applying the text color code to hyperlinks throughout the website.

Replace #YOURCOLORHEXCODE With the hex code of the color that you want your hyperlinks to be. A hex code identifies an individual color in CSS in HTML. For example, #FFFFFF identifies white while #000000 identifies black. In our example, we want our link colors to be orange, so we're going to input the following hex color: #FFB561.

Our website specific CSS code to change the color of hyperlinks throughout the website is as follows:

a {color:#FFB561;}

This means that every hyperlink in our website is going to be colored orange. When you enter the CSS code into the textbox, the links on the screen to the right should change accordingly.

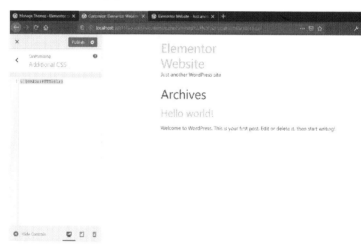

If you are pleased with the color, click the publish button, and close that tab (there's an X button in the top left). By now, you should have installed your theme, and set the color for your hyperlinks sitewide. Now it's time to install and configure all plugins.

Installing Plugins

Installing and configuring plugins is fairly simple and easy. All plugins will be installed via the WordPress repository, except for Elementor Pro which will need to manually be installed. Let's go through how to do that.

Plugins installed in one click:

- Elementor
- WordFence
- SendInBlue
- Envato Elements

The installation process is the same for each plugin, so we're going to use the Elementor plugin as an example. You follow the same steps for each of the four plugins mentioned above.

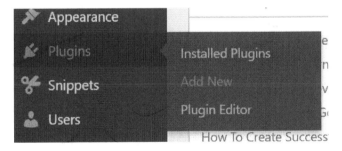

First, navigate to the add new plugins page and search for the respective plugin using the search box in the upper right hand corner.

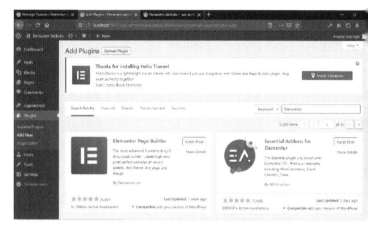

Then, identify the individual plugin, and click the install now button within the card. Clicking the install now button will automatically download the files necessary to run the plugin on to your WordPress website from the WordPress plugin repository. Once the plugin is installed, click the activate button.

Repeat the process for all the necessary plugins to your website (other than Elementor Pro which will be installed manually).

You can review that all of your plugins are successfully installed and activated by going to the installed plugins page, and comparing it to this following screenshot:

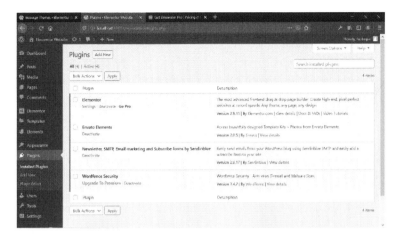

Once you have confirmed that all the free plugins are properly installed to your website, it's time to install Elementor Pro. Because Elementor Pro is a paid plugin, you need to install it a bit differently.

Manually Installing Plugins

the first thing you need to do is purchase the plugin. You do this through the Elementor Official Website. If you access that website through our link, a random discount code may be applied:

https://isotropic.co/out/Elementor

Depending on what you are looking to do, there are two pricing plans that you should be looking at period the first pricing plan comes in at a current price of $49.00 per year and allows you to install Elementor Pro onto 1 installation of WordPress. If you're only going to build one individual website in the coming year, you should opt for this plan.

If you are looking to build multiple websites using Elementor Pro, then purchase the $99 per year plan because it allows you to install Elementor Pro onto 3 individual WordPress installations. This could be helpful if you're building several websites for your company. For example, you may have your main corporate website, and then another individual website that advertises a specific service or subsidiary.

In most cases, the $49.00 per year plan is probably the right one for you. It offers all of the same features as the $99 per year plan, except only allows you to install Elementor Pro onto one website. You may see the expert plan which allows you to spend $200 per year and access 1000 installations of Elementor Pro. If you are going to create many websites with Elementor, this is the plan for you, and it's tailored specifically towards agencies and larger companies that have a need for incorporating a page builder into multiple websites.

Something that we should mention is that our agency subscribes to multiple "Expert Plans". we subscribe to these plans an install Elementor Pro into our client web sites. Sometimes, we have an excess of our licenses, which we resell to consumers just like you.

We resell these licenses anywhere from 5 to $15 depending on demand. If you are looking to save money on your subscription to Elementor Pro, feel free to reach out: hello@isotropic.co. Identify that you're coming from our E book, and would like to inquire about a resold Elementor Pro license.

Once you purchase the plugin, you will get a zip file download. Download that zip file onto your computer. Then navigate to your WordPress installation, and go to the add new plugin screen.

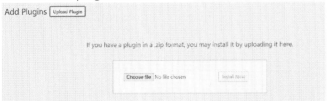

On the individual screen, right next to the main header, there is in upload plugin button. Click on the upload plugin button, and then upload the zip file that you downloaded from your Elementor Pro purchase.

Once the plugin is uploaded into the website, click the blue activate button, and all of the essential plugins for your WordPress and Elementor website will be active. Now, it's time to configure each individual plugin, and then get into building your actual website.

Why Opt For Pro?

It's probably at this point in the book that you realize that Elementor Pro costs about $50 per year. For some, that's an easy amount of money to invest in a good page builder. For others, that may be a large quantity of money, so you'll want to know exactly why upgrading to the pro version of this plugin is necessary.

Most of the features that we discuss in this book are only accessed via Elementor Pro. While it would be nice if the company offered all of the features for free, the developer team behind Elementor needs to get paid too. To get paid, they lock all of the useful features behind a paywall (which is the Pro version). In our opinion, the $49.00 per year price is extremely worth it.

if you were building a WordPress website without Elementor, you would need to probably purchase the following essential plugins. Here's a list of the industry-leading plugins and their costs:

- Forms: Gravity Forms, From $49.00/year (though to access the same features that Elementor Pro offers, you would probably need to opt for the $99 per year plan)
- Portfolio: $29-69.00/year
- Popups: Green Popups, $24.00/year
- Page Animations: There are many free plugins that will allow you to do this, but they require a lot of tinkering and would add hours to your workflow.

When you purchase Elementor Pro, you get all of these functionalities built in. The solutions that Elementor offers rival these individual plugins, and in most cases or even better than the standalone solutions. $192/year vs $49/year, Elementor wins pretty much every time. Obviously, there are some cases in which Elementor is not a good idea. For example, if you simply need a very simple single page website (which we wouldn't recommend in any circumstance), Elementor may be a bit overkill. At the same time, if you need a completely custom website with tons of custom functionality is, you would want to hire an agency to build you a website with WordPress, custom PHP, and custom plugins. However, for 98% of use cases, Elementor allows you to access a powerful visual page builder, create the website yourself, and replace multiple paid plugins with a single solution.

So with Elementor Pro, you get a ton of features that would normally require individual standalone plugin solutions, and you also get a ton of additional features and functionality within the page builder. Not to mention that the page builder itself is the most powerful in the industry, has the best community surrounding it, and allows you to visually build websites without needing to know code or hire an agency (which would cost into the thousands or $10,000s).

Configuring Elementor

Now that both of our free and premium plugins are installed onto our WordPress website, it's time to begin configuring everything. The first plugins we need to configure are the Elementor plugins. Elementor and Elementor Pro integrate together, so there's only one settings panel on the back end of the website for both of them.

The first thing you need to do is connect your license for Elementor Pro. This will enable all of the features better included with Elementor Pro and is a necessary thing to do.

License Settings

Activate License

Please activate your license to get feature updates, premium support and unlimited access to the template library.

Connect & Activate

All you need to do is navigate to Elementor, license, and then click on the connect and activate button. It will then have you connect to your Elementor website account, that you set up when you purchased the plug-in. Once you connect your development website to the Elementor license, you'll be able to access all of the features that element or pro has to offer.

If you need further assistance in activating your copy of Elementor Pro, check out this knowledge base article: https://docs.Elementor.com/article/333-license

For Elementor, the license is the only setting that you'll need to configure before building your website. When we migrate the website to a live host, we're going to have to go back into the settings and change a couple things, but for now it's time to configure WordFence.

Configuring WordFence

WordFence is the plugin that provides active security on our WordPress website. You could choose to install and activate this plugin once you have moved the website to a live domain but installing and activating WordPress on the development website ensures that there is proper protection, and all aspects of the website will work with WordFence.

Clicking on the WordFence menu item on the left-hand admin menu in WordPress will bring you to the setup wizard. Here, you need to enter your email, agree to the terms and conditions, and configure the scanning and web application firewall.

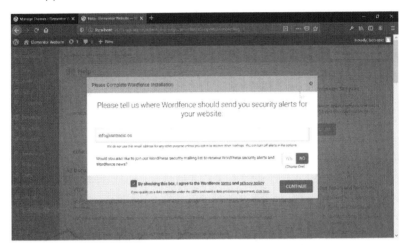

The tool will try to upsell you on WordFence premium, which while it's a good product, it's not necessary for a simple corporate website.

Now, the two things that we need to configure are they scanning and web application firewall capabilities.

If you haven't optimized the firewall, you'll be getting this message in the header of your admin interface for word press. Click on the configuration button to begin the configuration of the firewall.

Follow the steps in the configuration wizard, and make sure that the firewall is properly optimized. This is important because it will protect your website against hackers and additional threats. What it does is compares IP addresses to a large list of known hackers. If the IP address is a match, the hacker will be blocked from your website and unable to do anything malicious. The firewall will also block brute force attacks, which is the most common way hackers will gain access to your website.

You don't need to configure anything for the scans, though we recommend running a scan to understand how it works. To do this, go to the scan tab under the WordFence menu, and click the start a new scan button.

The tool will then automatically scan all the files on your WordPress website for any malicious items. In this case, there will be no issues because this is a brand new installation of WordPress. We recommend running a scan every week and making sure that all the files are clean. If the tool finds any malicious files, it will alert you, and attempt to remove them from your server.

Configuring SendInBlue

Now, we need to configure SendInBlue which will enable all notifications from your website to be sent via STMP. STMP is an email sending protocol, and installing this plugin will make sure that all notification emails will end up in your inbox. The default way WordPress usually identified by email providers like Gmail as spam. If you don't set this plugging up (or another plugin that does the same thing) you will probably end up missing vital form notifications, and security alerts.

The setup process is fairly simple with this plugin. First, you need to create a new account with SendInBlue. clicking on the create a new account button will direct you to the third party website, or you can create a free account. We previously stated in this book, but you can access 200 free emails per day. As long as you aren't receiving over 200 form notifications per day, the free plan is perfect for you.

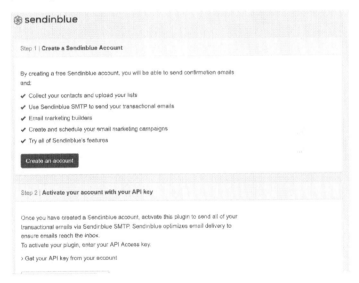

Once you've created an account on their service, do Step 2 which involves accessing an API key, and pasting it into the plugin user interface. To get to your API key, click on the "get your API key from your account" link.

Clicking on that link will load the API user interface from the third party SendInBlue application.

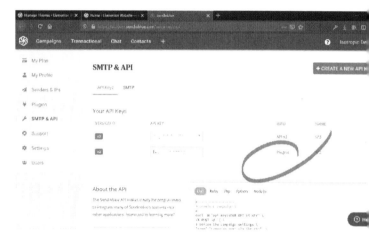

From this page, you'll want to copy the version two API key , and paste it into the "Access Key" Field on the plug in settings. Once the V2 key is pasted into the settings field, click the login button, and you should successfully see A screen that shows you your personal account information.

From this screen, the final thing to do is set up transactional emails. Transactional emails refer to all of the mail that will be sent from your website.

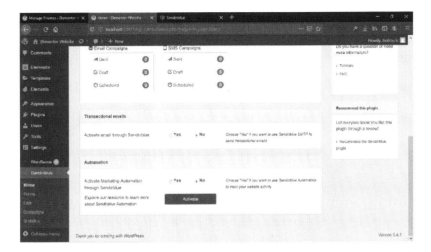

Toggle the "no" radio button to the "yes" radio button for transactional emails. Once activated, this service will send all emails leaving your WordPress website from their servers which ensures that they will end up in your inbox.

You can test that the emails from your WordPress website work by entering an email to send a test message to. Click the send email button, and that message should end up in the inbox of the address. If it works, you have properly configured the plugin, and your WordPress website will send emails correctly.

Configuring Envato Elements

The final plugin to configure is Envato Elements. This is the plugin that offers the 150 plus free website design templates, which we will be using when building the individual pages for the website.

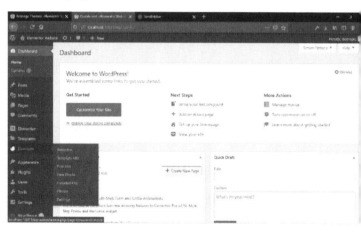

On the left hand admin menu, click on the elements tab. On the welcome page, select free templates kit. You can also opt for the premium templates kit, which are paid, but offer you a much larger selection. In this book we're going to be using free templates, which are installed and configured the same as premium templates.

If you end up on the "free templates kit" page, and see a collection of templates, this plugin is properly configured and installed.

The other two essential plugins that we mentioned in a previous section of this book are Breeze & Rank Math. We will be configuring both of these plugins on the production version of the website, as having a domain connected and being on the final version of the website hosting will aid in the configuration process of both of these plugins.

We'll be coming back to these plug-ins very soon, but first let's get into the actual building of the website. Our initial step when creating a website is going to be the header in the footer. From there, we're going to select a template that works well with our website, and then design the actual pages.

We create these websites in this specific order, but you can switch some of the steps around. For example, you can choose your templates before creating the header in the footer. In our use case, will create a header and footer, select a template, and then go back to the header and footer and make sure it works well with the website.

When building any website, especially with a visual builder, the process is very circular. You're going to flow between multiple steps going forwards and backwards which will ensure that you end up with the best final product. Revision and feedback when it comes to website design is extremely important. You'll want to offer yourself feedback, and revise upon aspects of the website that you identify need work period you also want third party feedback, from both your employees and your customers.

Creating Your Header & Footer

Before designing the actual header, we're going to create a placeholder menu that we can use when styling the header. This placeholder menu will identify the basic pages that we're going to create on this website, and will eventually be replaced by a menu of the same design that is actually functional.

To create the placeholder menu, navigate to appearances and then menu.

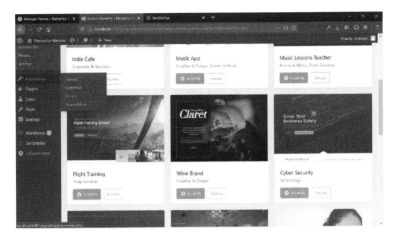

Most of the time, there will be a placeholder menu that is already created for you. We typically will rename this menu to "placeholder menu", delete the existing page entries, and then add our own.

We add our own links by going to the custom links section and entering a page name and URL address.

If you want your menu to become functional as you create the pages, and already know what your URL is going to be for each individual page, you can save time by adding links that will soon be functional.

If you don't know what your page structure is going to be, then you can simply input "#".

When creating the menu, use the website address of your local installation. In our case, the root website URL for our local installation is http://localhost:10011/. that means that the custom URL of our homepage is going to be http://localhost:10011/. An example URL for a sub page would be http://localhost:10011**/about** -- that would link the user to the **about page**.

If you opt to use your own links, don't use your final domain address. In our case, the domain address that this website will be live on is (We will review how to purchase, and set up this domain at a later section in this book) However, instead of the final domain address we're going to be using the http://localhost:10011/ address, which will make the menu functional on our local installation. When we migrate the website from the local installation to the live host, this address will automatically be replaced with our live domain address (We will be discussing the migration process at a later point in this book).

To create an individual menu item, go to the custom links tab, enter the URL (or # if you're doing a placeholder), menu item title, and then click add to menu.

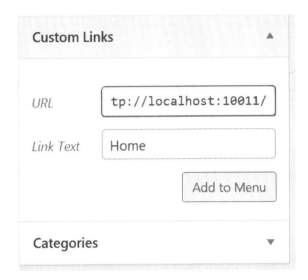

Because we already know the pages that we're going to be using in this example website, we're going to add links that will work as soon as we create the individual page. So, here are the URLs and link texts for all of our pages:

- Home | http://localhost:10011/
- Services | http://localhost:10011/services
- About | http://localhost:10011/about
- Blog | http://localhost:10011/blog
- Contact | http://localhost:10011/contact

After adding all these menu items, the menu user interface should look like this. Make sure to save your menu (click Create Menu).

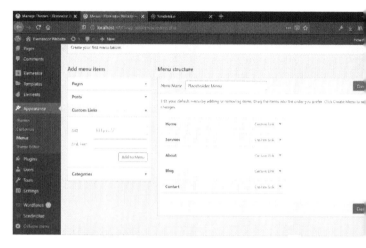

If you need more information on creating menus in WordPress, check out this guide: https://codex.wordpress.org/WordPress_Menu_User_Guide

Now that our main menu is created, let's go ahead and begin building our header.

Header

Before building the header, we need to determine what it's design will be. The typical header design has your business logo on the left, while the menu lies on the right. We recommend using the typical header design, because users are familiar with it, and it's a simple and proven interface device for websites.

You can make your header more complex by adding a top bar or a call to action. If you're a small business that offers a local service, it's a good idea to include contact information in your header, so we're going to use a top bar to do that. We're also going to add a call to action "request a quote" but you can leave out any or all of these elements if you feel that your business won't benefit from them.

If you would like to read an in-depth article on the best practices for website header design, check out this post: https://uxplanet.org/website-header-design-in-2020-best-practices-and-examples-1992f80ddd69

You should also consider whether you want your menu to be fixed or sticky. A fixed menu is fixed to the top of the page. When the user scrolls, the menu will scroll with the page. A sticky menu is not fixed to the top of the page, and when the user scrolls, the menu will stay at the top of the screen, and overlay the content. There are pros and cons for both approaches, but we're going to design our website with a fixed menu. Using a fixed menu also makes the design and development of it a bit more simple.

Now that we know what our basic header is going to look like, let's go ahead and create it.

To begin the creation of our menu, go to templates, and then theme builder. The included theme builder with Elementor Pro allows you to visually edit aspects of your website that were typically out of bounds for every day users (think headers, footers, and page/post templates). Typically, users could only change these elements of their website by changing the entire theme behind it.

The theme builder has three main components:

Template Type – Choose the type of template you want to create. This can be header, footer, single post page or archive page.

Dynamic data – Build the framework of your page using dynamic content. This way, your content gets filled dynamically with content from your website

Conditions – Set conditions to determine where your template will apply: across your website, for a specific page, or any condition you may like

Let's make out header with this builder:

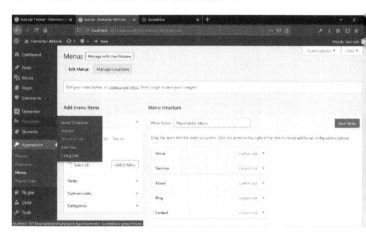

Click add new, and set your template type to be header. Label your template "main header".

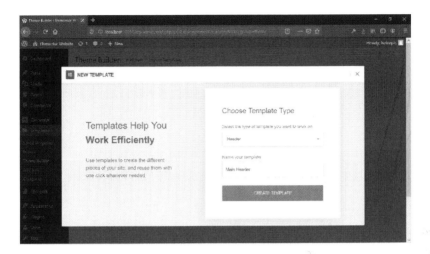

You should have identified the brand guidelines, typography, and colors in the previous section of this book. This will be the first implementation of these aspects of your website. When you load the page builder for your header, the first thing you will be greeted with is a collection of templates that you can use to build your menu.

Using templates to build your menu is a great idea because it will save you time. For this example, we're going to build the menu from scratch so you can understand the basic features of the page builder, and what you can do with it.

The first thing you need to do is add a main section for your header. This first section will contain the logo, and menu.

Click the pink plus button on the canvas screen, and select the structure of your main section. Our structure is going to have a smaller column on the left (20% width), and the larger column on the right (80% width).

We're going to select the 50/50 structure, and then individually set the percentage with of each column within the section.

Before we set the width of the column, let's set the background of the menu. In this example, we're going to make our menu background white. To do this, hover over the section, go to the blue tab, and right click on the 2nd icon that is displaying. This will toggle a right click menu, and from it click on edit section.

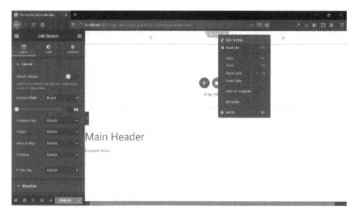

Clicking on edit section will make the left hand page builder user interface show all settings that relate to the individual section. To change the background color of the section, go to the style tab.

In the style section, go to the background tab, select classic, and then set your background color.

Once we've edited the main section background, edit the column to the left by right clicking on it and clicking edit column.

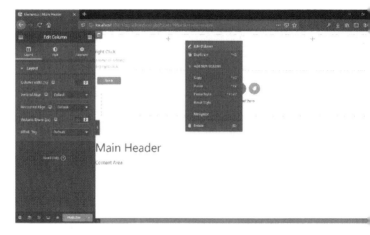

The first option in the edit column section of the page builder is column width. Set this column width to be 20%. This will automatically make the left column 20% of the screen width and the right column will be 80% of the screen width.

Now it's time to add the first elements to your website with the Elementor page builder. The first thing we're going to add to our menu is a business logo on the left hand side. From the page builder elements panel, find an image element, and drag and drop it into the left hand column. Then, set your image by clicking on the individual image, uploading your logo to the website, and applying it to the image.

Now, we want to add in our page menu. Go back to the elements view of the page builder panel, Search for nav menu, and then drag and drop the menu into the right hand column.

The placeholder menu should automatically be populated into this section. Set the alignment of the menu to right. There are many options that you can change related to the menu, but the main things you should focus on are the color of the text, and the typography (font, sizing) of the individual menu elements. To change the color and typography, go to the style section in the page builder, and manipulate the respective options. To learn more about the options and features behind the individual navigation menu, check out this article:

https://docs.Elementor.com/article/244-nav-menu

You will also want to change the active and hover colors of the individual menu. If you hover over the default menu on the canvas beside the page builder user interface, you will see that the individual items highlight green when your mouse runs over them. To change this color to match your branding, go to Edit Nav Menu, Style → Hover → Pointer/Text Color, and set the colors to your specifications.

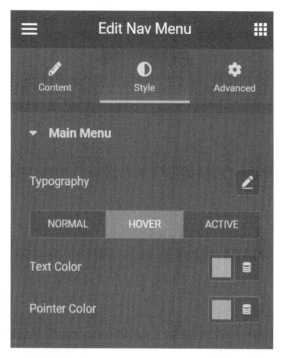

By now, we have a super simple header set up for our future website. The one additional thing that we want to add to this menu is a top bar that contains our phone number and email address. To do this, we're going to add a new section to the web page, set the background color of the section to be blue, drag the section above the main header section, and then add a text editor element to it.

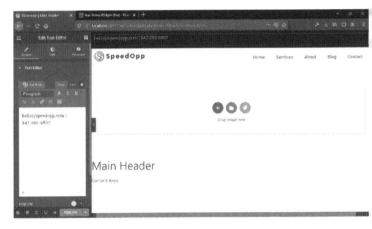

In the text editor user interface, we're going to type in our email address and phone number. You can choose to make these links by highlighting each individual form of contact and inputting Ctrl+K. This will set an email link (mailto:email@email.com) and telephone link (tel:1231231234) in the underlying html.

Now, we're going to set it to be aligned to the right of the screen and change the font color to white.

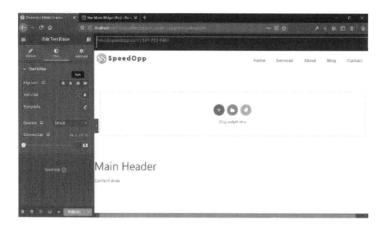

You may notice that there is an uneven spacing with this individual text element. The bottom has around a 15 pixel (px) space, compared to the top, where there is a five pixel space. This spacing is by design with Elementor, because when you have large text blocks, having a space beneath them makes the content more readable. However, when you're implementing it in this use case, this space is not necessary.

To remove the 15 pixel spacing on the bottom of the text element, navigate to the advanced features tab in the Elementor page builder. Then, set the margin bottom to be -15px. the rest of the margins should be set to be 0, and you can change an individual margin by deselecting the link icon.

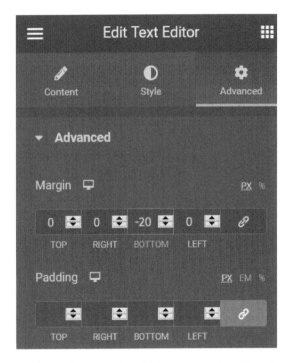

At this point, we should have a working header for our website that can be applied to all pages. Here's what our basic header looks like:

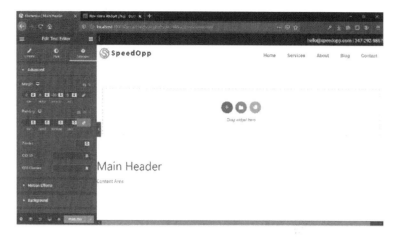

Because this is a visual builder, you can include whatever you want in the menu. For example, if you'd like to include a call to action (ie. "Request A Quote"), you can easily do that by dragging and dropping an Elementor button into the menu, labeling it and styling it accordingly.

Now that our menu is complete, we're going to publish it and apply it to all pages on the website period to do this, hit the big green publish button in the bottom of the Elementor page builder user interface. Clicking the publish button will toggle the display conditions menu. Click the add condition button and set your header to apply to the entire website.

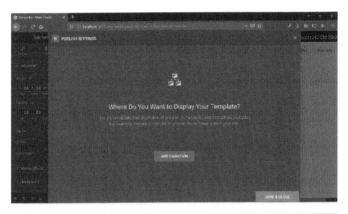

This is a very powerful functionality that we want to
introduce to you in this section. Display conditions
allows you to create multiple versions of headers,
footers, and any other template that Elementor allows
you to create, and then display it on specific sections
and categories of your website. For example, if we
created a menu and wanted to display it only on our
blog posts, while displaying another menu (styled
differently than the first) on our main pages, we could
do so.

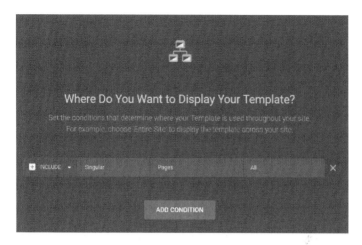

For example, this setup would apply our menu to all singular pages on our website. We could then set another menu to apply to all singular blog posts on our website.

This tool allows us to specify the application of individual templates down to a page/post level.

For this example website, we're going to apply this menu to every single page, post, archive, and view of our website (include Entire Site).

With the display conditions set, click the save and close button, and the header will now be live on your website. You can check the application of the template by navigating to the root URL of your website and checking to see if the header is displaying.

Remember, that you could have started off with a template which would save you the trouble of having to create sections and elements. If you did the template route, you would be able to simply change the content in the existing structure to match your own branding.

We definitely recommend this method, and the only reason we showed you the individual build process of this menu was to introduce you to the page builder, the functionalities behind it, and the basic elements. For the rest of this book, we're going to be using the templates.

For the footer, we're going to create a super simple single line folder That displays our company name, Copyright, and contact email. If you would like to make a complicated footer with links, sign up forms, and more, this is very simple to do using a template. Simply select a footer that you like, and then style it accordingly using the principles and techniques that we just outlined.

Make the footer by going to the back end of your WordPress website (wp-admin), and then heading over to templates, theme builder, creating a new template, naming it and setting it to be the footer, and then building your footer. Remember, using a template will speed up your footer creation process immensely. You do this by following the same workflow outlined when creating the menu.

Once you have finished creating your footer, click the publish button, apply the footer to the entire website, and then check the front end to make sure it shows.

Now that we have our basic header and footer created for our entire website, it's time to begin building the pages.

Using Templates

Before building the pages, we're going to introduce the main templates to you, and explain why using templates is a great idea.

We've pushed the pros and cons of templates throughout this book, but in this section we're going to consolidate all of our thoughts into one place.

As a small business owner, your main priority should be focusing on what your company actually does. So, if you sell handbags, you want to be focusing on selling handbags, and if you run a veterinary practice, you want to be focused on veterinarian services, not building a website.

If you fall into this category (SBO), and you don't want to hire a third party to create your website (which is perfectly valid), your top priority should be creating a super well designed website that generates leads and credibility, *in the least amount of time possible*.

The chances are that you're not a professional designer, and that there are some tips and tricks that you don't know yet for Elementor. Instead of spending hours and days learning how to create pages, modifying pre existing examples will save you a lot of time and struggle.

There are multiple sources of templates for Elementor. An individual template can be downloaded onto your website, and automatically insert sections, columns, placeholder text, images and more to get to the final product of a complete web page.

From this complete page, you will be able to change images to match your business, change text to match your content, change all of the colors and more. However, the underlying structure of the page is there. This saves you the time of having to go and build an entire web page, and there are templates for every page on the website from the home page to the contact page.

Another big benefit of using templates is that they are typically professionally designed, and really well put together. Not only will they look good, but they will effectively convey the message of your business, and you won't need to dedicate days to wireframing, planning and getting third party feedback on your page designs.

From the process of editing text and changing specific items on the page, you'll grow to understand how to use Elementor Pro, and will eventually become proficient in creating your own pages if need be. This is why we recommend using templates now, and then as your skills and confidence grow with the tool, you can create your own pages if need be.

Elementor Pro comes pre bundled with over 100 individual templates that are professionally designed. These are super easy and simple to insert into your website, and come pre built into the page builder. however, because Elementor has over 5 million installations, many websites already used these templates.

You want your website to stand out from the pack, so we recommend using a third-party template provider called Envato Elements. You should have already installed the plugin when we installed the essential plugins for the website, which means that the templates are now active on your website. Let's run through how to use this plugin, download templates, and then discuss creating the actual pages in your website.

From your WordPress admin backend, click on the elements tab in the left hand menu. This will load the user interface for the Envato Elements plugin, and you'll be able to scroll through the 150 free templates (and if you choose purchase a premium add-on which gives you access to a lot more).

In this section and the remainder of the book, we're going to be building our website with a specific template. However, the process of installing templates, on both the website and the specific page doesn't change, so you can end up choosing whatever template you want. You can even go with the included templates in Elementor Pro, as the installation process is remarkably similar.

If you navigate to the free templates tab, you will be greeted with a current selection of 150 template kits, and over 2000 individual templates.

A template kit is a complete website with multiple pages within it. Think of a kit as a folder of individual templates.

By using a template kit throughout the website, you will have a standard design style that you can base your customizations off of.

The first step to using a template is to install it into the website. By clicking the install button on the template, you'll end up downloading the files that make up this template, which will then be able to insert into specific Elementor pages. You can use the search feature of the plugin to find industries that are the same as the one that your business occupies. For example, if you're a plumber, searching for "plumber" will return all template kits that were designed for those operating in that sector.

You can also sort the individual template kits by category, and each category relates to a specific industry. In our example, we're going to be taking a look at the "trade services" category and building a website for an example plumber.

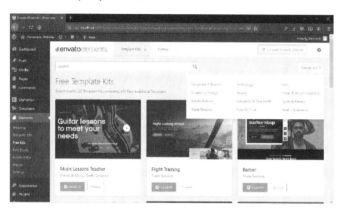

In many cases, there won't be a template that is specifically created for what your business does. However, that's not to worry about because you're going to be changing all of the images and text within the template. When browsing through templates, you want to look at the underlying structure of each page. Do you like how this page presents information? Do you like how the website is actually styled?

If you like the individual thumbnail, clicking on the preview button beside the install kit button, will load an interface where you can explore all of the individual templates contained within the kit.

When you load the preview page, you will be greeted with full page screenshots of every individual template contained within the kit. There are usually multiple versions of a single page. In this example, you have three versions of the home page to choose from. Clicking on the full page screenshot will load the actual template in HTML and CSS.

You can even preview the individual page on different screen sizes which correspond to desktop sizes, tablet sizes, and mobile sizes. On the topic of responsiveness, all of these templates are designed to work on the three major devices, meaning you won't need to worry about each individual version of the page. (Mobile responsiveness is important! In the next section we're going to review the responsive design tools that Elementor has to offer you.)

You may also notice that these templates don't come with headers and footers. That's why we created a header in a footer in the beginning steps of this section of our book. Creating the header and footer not only gives you a good understanding of how to use basic features in the page builder, but it also allows you to view your entire page as the public would as soon as you install a template. If you create your header and footer at a later step in this book, you won't be able to preview it within the visual builder.

If you have determined that this template is a good fit for your website, it's time to install it to your WordPress installation.

That's a fairly simple thing to do: all you need to do is go back to your WordPress admin back-end, go onto the Envato Elements plugin, find your individual template kit card, and click the green install button.

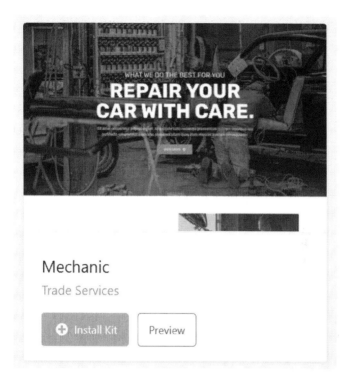

Mechanic

Trade Services

Install Kit | Preview |

Once your template has successfully been installed onto your WordPress website, you may get a notice on the back end editor stating that you need to install required packages for this template to work.

Missing Requirements

Please install and activate these missing requirements for this Template Kit to work correctly. We recommend checking with your web developer before applying these changes.

☑ Setting: Elementor default color schemes ✅ *Success!*
☑ Setting: Elementor default typography schemes ✅ *Success!*
☑ Custom CSS: These styles are added to the WordPress Customizer. Preview CSS ✅ *Success!*
❶ FYI: This Template Kit has only been tested with the "Hello Elementor" WordPress theme. If the imported templates don't look correct please read this article.

Once the above is completed you can close this window.

[➕ Close]

Typically, these requirements are default color schemes, custom typography, and custom CSS. These are installed automatically on to the website. If you read through the missing requirements photo above, you'll see that this template kit has only been tested with hello Elementor. Pretty much every template created for Elementor is created to be used with this theme, which is why we installed it in the previous section in this book.

Now that our requirements are installed, it's time to go ahead and create the actual pages.

Creating the Actual Pages

Instead of reviewing step by step how to create each individual page, and edit all aspects of it, we're going to be introducing you to the three major pages in your website, and teaching you techniques that you can use across all pages in your website. By the end of this section, you should understand how to install templates, how to build a homepage, a blog page, and a contact page, *and* be able to carry these skills over to any other page you may need (like an about page, services page, history page, or more).

We're going to start on creating the homepage, and then discussed the blog page, and then finally discussed the contact page.

Home

As stated in previous sections in this book, the home page is an important first impression, and one that should lead visitors to where they want to go. To build the homepage, you'll need to know what other pages you'll be including in your website.

There are a couple things that you want to lookout for when building a home page. The first thing is that you don't want to overload the homepage with tons of text. Lots of small words are typically glossed over by visitors even if they contain meaningful and helpful information. On a home page, you want to include large headers, and short descriptions beneath them.

You can save your large amounts of content for other pages like these services page or about page. This homepage is simply created to funnel visitors to those individual pages previewed for example, if you have a visitor who ends up on your website and wants to understand more about what your company has to offer, You want there flow through the home page to look something like this:

- End up on page
- Validate that they are on the right page by looking at the header logo and hero header text

- Scroll down and view a headline that says services
- read the description
- click on the button and end up on the services page where they can read in depth about what your company has to offer

You don't want your user to end up on the page and then not understand where to go from there.

Now that we understand the basic purpose and structure of a homepage, let's discuss what goes into actually creating the page, from inserting the template to changing the content.

The first step of creating the homepage is creating the actual page within WordPress. To do this, go to pages, and then add new.

This should load the Gutenberg block editor (default editor for Pages & Posts in WordPress), where you will input necessary page information, check that everything is in order, and then load the Elementor page builder.

The first thing you want to do is title your page home and then save it as a draft. Once you've titled your page, set the featured image, tag the page, and save it again. now you're ready to launch the Elementor page builder period to do this, click edit with Elementor, which is a blue button on the top bar of the Gutenberg block editor.

Edit with Elementor

The Elementor page builder will initialize, and in a few seconds, you'll be greeted with the user interface.

When building any main page, the first thing to do is toggle the page title off. You'll probably see a title that says "home" on the page. Turning this title off makes everything look a lot cleaner, and more professional period to do this, go to page settings, and then toggle the page title off.

Now that the page title is off, we're ready to insert our first page template.

To do this click the third green icon in the main canvas area of the page. This will initialize the Envato Elements user interface, where you can insert specific pages into your builder. When the popup loads, you'll see the template kit that you have installed at a previous point in this process.

Clicking on the individual template kit thumbnail will load all the pages that are contained within it.

Once you've identified the page that you want to insert (in our case it is going to be home page template #3), Click on insert template. After a few seconds, the template will be inserted into your page, and the popup will close.

By now you should have a fully functional, completely built home page inserted into your website. From this point, it's time to change the actual content within the page to match your company. We recommend changing everything possible from the images to the text to the colors.

Let's review how to change a couple aspects of this website. For example, from the photo above, you can see that there are a bunch of text elements, a blue circle, and a background image. Let's change all of these. First, we don't really like how the blue circle looks on the website, so we're going to delete it. This is fairly simple to do all you need to do is right click on the blue circle and then click the delete button in the menu.

Changing the actual text in Elementor is a very simple and easy thing to do. Simply find the text that you want to change, click on it, delete the placeholder, and enter your own. You can do this on the canvas itself or within the left-hand section on the page builder. We're going to be changing this website to mirror a plumber, so all of the existing placeholder text will be changed accordingly.

When it comes to buttons, you can change the actual label of the button from the canvas. Clicking on the text label will initialize the editor, and you can simply delete the placeholder an add your own text. In this example we're going to keep the text for the button on the homepage but change the link to match our page structure.

In this example, we want this button to lead to the services page. we know that our services page is going to be hosted at http://localhost:10011/services, So we can enter that link in the button even if that page doesn't exist yet. Keep in mind that we're using the local installation root domain, which will automatically be replaced when we migrate the website to a live server.

To change the link of a button, you can do this by changing the second input box on the page builder user interface When the button is selected. You can select the button by simply clicking on it. Also, hovering over any element and clicking on the upper right hand icon that displays will initialize the settings within the page builder for that specific element as well.

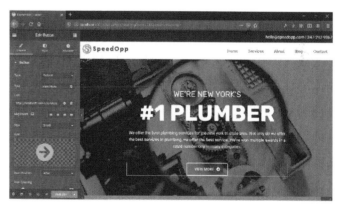

To change the background image, you need to edit the element that the image is a background for. In this example, the first section on the page is what houses the background image.

Hover over the main section, and click on the center button in the blue tab that display is. This will initialize the section settings within the page builder interface.

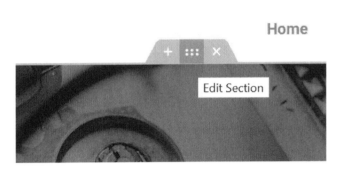

You'll see that this section has many custom settings that were preset when you installed the template into the page. In this example, the only thing we want to do is change the background image for this section, and to do this we need to go to the style tab in the page builder interface.

Under the background section of the style tab, you'll see that the background image is set to be the current placeholder. Hovering over that image in the page builder interface and clicking change image will initialize the WordPress media library. Simply upload the image that is specific to your company, we suggest a photo of your team or a photo of your company and click insert photo. That will replace the placeholder photo with your business specific one.

The best part about the visual page builder is that you can preview your changes in real time. If the image changes, you know that you've successfully changed the image background on the front end as well.

Now, all you need to do is run through the rest of the template and change all of the placeholder content to content that matches your company. You can also choose to add and remove sections as you need.

There are a few general rules of thumb when it comes to editing existing sections with Elementor. If the main section has a background color that you would like to change to match your branding guidelines, clicking on the section, going to the style tab, and then editing the background color is the way to change that main color.

If there is a text element that you would like to change style wise, you do this by clicking on the text element, going to the style tab within the Elementor page builder, and changing the respective setting.

If there is a spacing issue, and there shouldn't be, you can change it by editing the margin and the padding within the advanced setting section in the page builder.

If you are unable to click on an individual element (you would typically be doing this to edit the content that it contains), Elementor has included a very handy tool called "navigator".

On the bottom of the page builder user interface there are five individual icons that will toggle specific tools within the builder. The second icon will toggle the navigation popup.

This popup will allow you to view the actual structure of the page, but remove all visual aspects. It makes it easy to select any element. Additionally, you can drag and drop the elements within the navigator to rearrange them on the main page. Depending on how you work, this might be very helpful to you.

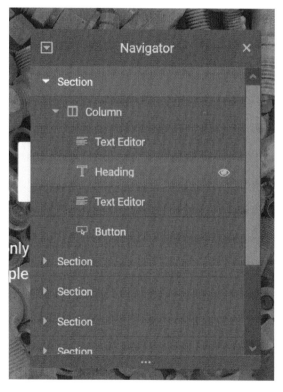

If you make any mistakes, you can simply undo it by doing control or command Z.

Elementor also tracks the revision history of your page. Have you published a version of your page several weeks ago that you would like to revert back to. You can do this by clicking on the third icon on the menu under the page builder interface (That would be the icon directly next to the navigator one).

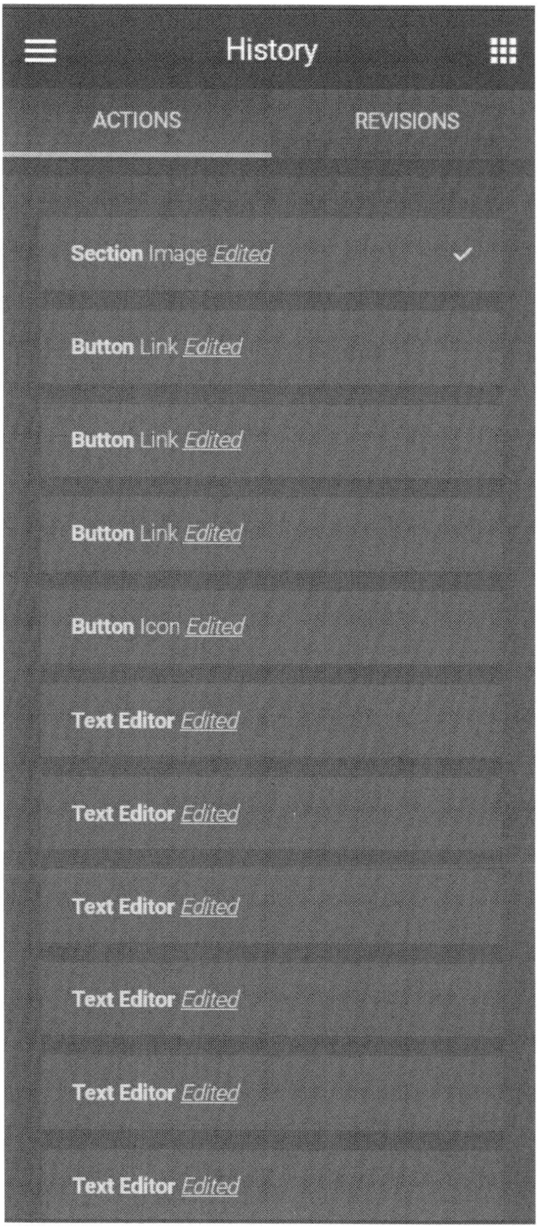

History

ACTIONS | REVISIONS

Section Image *Edited* ✓

Button Link *Edited*

Button Link *Edited*

Button Link *Edited*

Button Icon *Edited*

Text Editor *Edited*

Text Editor *Edited*

Text Editor *Edited*

Text Editor *Edited*

Text Editor *Edited*

Text Editor *Edited*

The first tab in the history section is called Actions. Actions displays every change you made to the page during the current session. It is basically a visual undo and redo interface. Clicking on an individual action will revert the page back to that action. If you look at the previous picture for an example, clicking on button icon would change the icon of a button and remove all changes before that.

If you would like to revert back to a previous version of the page, going to the revisions tab and selecting the version of the page depending on the date and time it was published will revert you back to that version.

Finally, (we discussed responsive design a bit earlier) but Elementor will allow you to view the page in desktop, tablet, and mobile format. If you're using a template, these are already designed to be mobile responsive, but you can check to make sure that everything is working by clicking on the 4th icon in the bottom menu which is the screen size changer.

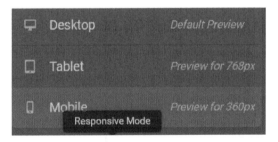

If you select the mobile screen size, the viewport in the canvas will change accordingly. This is really helpful when you need to make sure that your website will work on all devices. A little known statistic is the fact that 60% of your visitors will view your website from a mobile device. That's why making sure your website works and is usable on all screen sizes is absolutely essential to its success.

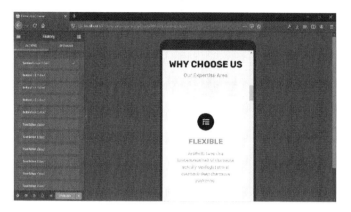

When you've finished editing your page, and assure that it works on all screen sizes and device types, it's time to publish it. Publish the page by clicking the big green publish button.

To view the changes on the front end, go to HTTPS://YOURROOTDOMAIN/HOME (http://localhost:10011/home is our example).

Once you've ensured that the page published correctly, it's time to set this as the default page that your website will load.

To do this, click the customize tab in the top bar. That will initialize the same loader that we used to change the color of the hyperlinks throughout the website. This time, go to the homepage settings tab.

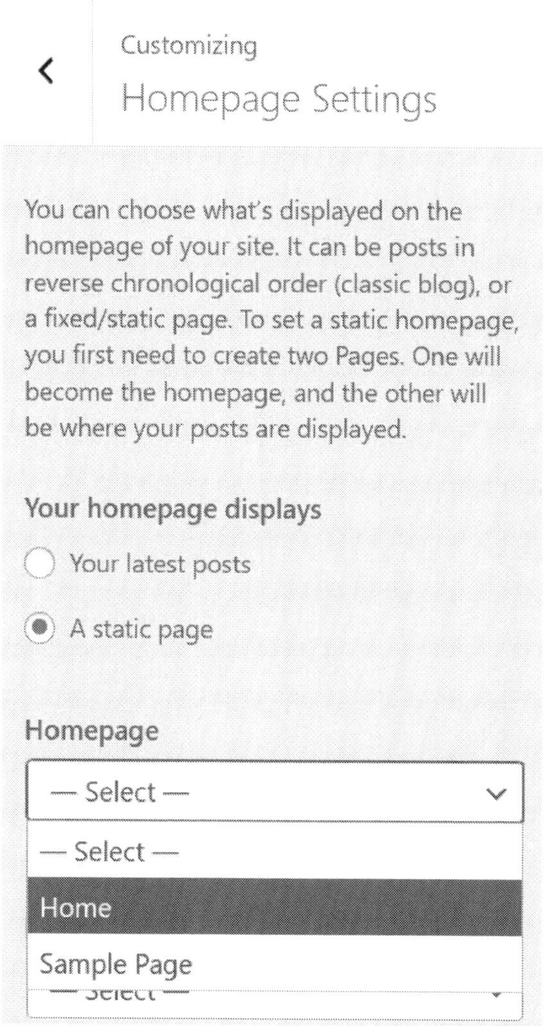

Homepage Settings

You can choose what's displayed on the homepage of your site. It can be posts in reverse chronological order (classic blog), or a fixed/static page. To set a static homepage, you first need to create two Pages. One will become the homepage, and the other will be where your posts are displayed.

Your homepage displays

○ Your latest posts

◉ A static page

Homepage

— Select — ⌄
— Select —
Home
Sample Page

Change the radio button from your latest post to a static page and then select the homepage to be "home". Now, your home page will load when you go to your root domain. Click the publish button, had to root domain, and ensure that the changes have been pushed to your live website.

On the topic of the Customiser, another thing you may want to change at this point is the Favicon of your website, and ensure that your website title and tagline are what you want them to be.

Favicon

The Favicon is the small icon that loads in a browser tab when a visitor is on your website. the typical Favicon is an icon of WordPress, and keeping it like this is unprofessional. To change it, under the site identity tab in the Customiser, and set both the logo and the site icon to match your brand. The site icon is what directly impacts the Favicon, and should be 512 pixels by 512 pixels (though any size that is square should work).

Once you change it, you'll get a preview of what it will look like on the front end of your website. If you like what it looks like, click the publish button in the upper right hand corner of the Customiser interface, and then close the tab.

Site Icon

*Site Icons are what you see in browser tabs,
bookmark bars, and within the WordPress
mobile apps. Upload one here!*

*Site Icons should be square and at least 512 ×
512 pixels.*

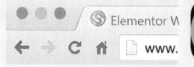

Now that we've created our homepage, set it as the
default page for our website, and ensured that our
Favicon was properly set, let's go ahead and create our
blog page.

Before we create the blog page, understand that all of
the topics discussed in creating a home page, from
importing a template to changing the button text and
links is the same workflow that you'll be using when
creating an about page, a services page, and any
additional pages you may need. That's why we're not
going to review the creation of each individual page in
this section, as the steps that you take to do so are the
same throughout.

You can choose to build your website in any order that
you feel fit, so we feel that creating the homepage, the
blog page, and the contact page first, and then going
ahead and making supporting pages such as a business
about page or services page is a good way to do things.

Blog

It's now time to make our blog page. Having a blog on your business website is beneficial in many ways. First, actively publishing content that users want to read will establish you as an expert in your field. Because people trust experts, your credibility goes up, and so does your lead generation. Additionally, if somebody reads an article about the service that you provide, and the needs the service at a later point, they'll remember that you were the person / company that educated them on the topic, come back to your website, and fill out a contact form.

Publishing a blog is also a very good idea when it comes to SEO. Having an active website that grows, has relevant keywords , and that people link to will push its overall rankings in Google up. If you rank higher in Google, you'll have more inbound traffic, and more of that inbound traffic will convert to leads.

Creating a blog doesn't need to be difficult, and all you need for SEO is about 600 words per week that is relevant and well written. You can choose to hire a SEO marketing company to do this for you, or you can bang out a 600 word article in 10 minutes yourself.

In this section of the book, we're going to discuss how to create a blog with Elementor. There are two main parts to a blog. Archive pages, and individual blog posts. We need to create page templates that apply to each of these, as the content in them changes dynamically, but the structure of each individual page remains standard.

We're going to discuss creating the archive page for your blog, then creating the template for your blog post, and then publishing individual blog posts from the back end of your website.

Archive

First up is your archive. To create the individual archive, you're going to go to templates, theme builder, and create a new template that applies to all archives on the website.

In some cases, the Envato Elements plugin may contain a template for your blog archive, but in many cases it doesn't. For the example template kit that we're using, there's no blog archive template. However, we're still big proponents of templates, and we're going to be using a standard Elementor Pro blog post template in this circumstance.

To add an Elementor Pro template, click on the grey folder icon in the initial canvas that loads.

Drag widget here

That will toggle the Elementor Pro templates interface. This is very similar to the Envato Elements template, except you don't need to install any kits from the back end of the website.

If you scroll through the templates that element or pro has to offer, you'll see that there are pre styled ones, and placeholder ones.

Archives

We're going to be using a pre styled template, and simply changing the colors and typography of it to match our existing template kit that we're using for all our other pages.

Depending on the template you choose, you'll be needing to edit and style different things. In our case, we needed to edit and style the text contained with the template.

The main aspects of any blog post archive page are the header, description, and archive posts:

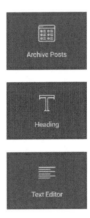

Most of the time, you'll want to be changing the font styles and colors. To do this you go to the style tab in the page builder interface, and from there, you can change all font colors, sizes and styles.

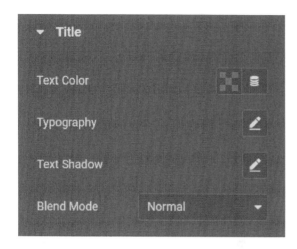

When you're ready to publish your blog post archive, simply click the green published button on the lower right hand corner of the interface, and set your display conditions to include all archives.

Once published, we need to set this to apply to our main blog post page. To do this, create a new page on the back end of the WordPress website, title it "blog" (This should also set the permalink to be yourdomain.com/blog), and publish it.

Now, navigate to the Customiser which can be accessed to be at the top bar from the front end of your website, go to homepage settings, and set your Posts Page to be the page that you just published.

Once these changes are made, go to the front end of the website, navigate to the blog URL, and ensure that your archive styling displays. If your archive style displays, you got this section right and it's time to create the individual blog post template.

Template
The individual template dictates the structure of a blog post. To make the blog post template, navigate to

Templates, theme builder, and create a new template that applies to a single post

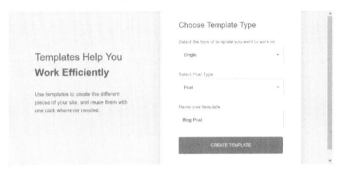

Now, the workflow is the same here as it was for your archive. Use an Elementor Pro or Envato Elements template to create your blog post structure. A typical blog post has a title, featured image, content, and then comments. Ensure that your template contains all of these elements. Here is a base template that we use for many of our blog posts throughout our websites:

ALICE STEVENS

8 Podcasts by Boss Women You Should Subscribe to Right Now

September 16, 2018 , 3:29 pm , Online Marketing

Lorem ipsum dolor sit amet, consectetur adipiscing elit. Etiam tempor intee suscipit feugiat semper. Ut venenatis libero sit amet ante in lobortis arcu mollis.

Companies and organizations are getting their hands on our data and using it for a number of reasons we don't even know about. Luckily, there are a number of things you can do to minimize your presence online and protect your privacy, without having to ditch the internet.

For starters, turn on incognito mode in your web browser. This disables the tracking tools in your browser and prevents websites from collecting your personal information. You can also block third-party cookies — cookies are small pieces of data that enable information about you to be remembered by external sites.

If you're a social media user, you've got a 46 percent higher risk of an account takeover or fraud compared to non-social media users. So it's important to set specific settings for your posts. For example, on Facebook you can limit access to your future posts to make sure they are only visible to your friends. You should also update your privacy settings to hide your personal information from your pages so random people can't access things including your email address or phone number. Lastly, make sure to block external apps from accessing your personal data.

SHARE THIS POST

0 Comments   Sort by Oldest ▾

Add a comment...

Facebook Comments Plugin

This can easily be inserted via the Elementor Pro templates library. All you need to do is change the color and the font family for the page.

You will probably want to style your blog post template to match the styling of other pages on your website. This typically involves changing font families, text, and colors.

Once you have built your blog post template, click the publish button, and apply to all blog post types (This should be the default option that loads with the popup).

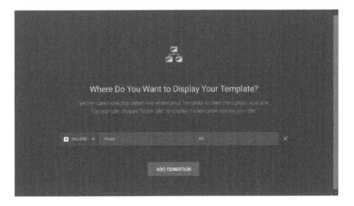

Publishing Posts

Now you have your archive that displays all of the blog posts that you have published, and your single post template that applies to all blog posts. The archive is the page that people will view when navigating to yoursite.com/blog, and then clicking on an individual post that is listed on the archive will bring them to the post template populated with the specific content for that blog post.

Let's talk about the process of actually publishing a blog post.

The process of creating a blog post is very similar to creating a new page within WordPress. All you need to do is go to posts, add new.

Simply add your title, content, featured image, and taxonomy settings, and then publish the post. If you have properly set up your archive and blog post templates, this post should display under the archive. When you click on its individual entry, the single blog post should load, styled to the specifications that you dictated in the single post template.

Gutenberg Vs Elementor

You may notice that we didn't suggest building the individual blog post with the Elementor builder. Instead, we used the default text editor that comes with modern versions of WordPress called Gutenberg. You may also notice that on the blog post there is an edit with Elementor button. That means that if you want to, you can create a blog post with the Elementor page builder (it would be the same workflow as creating a page, except your single post template would be applied to it).

Unless you are building an extremely complex blog post that requires many design elements, we would suggest you stay away from using the Elementor builder when creating blog posts.

This is because Elementor allows you to be extremely powerful with your design, but it also bloats your website with unnecessary code. You want your blog posts to load as fast as possible, and you want the visitors focus to be on the content at hand. The Gutenberg editor is a much leaner piece of software that outputs a lot cleaner code. In English, that means that your blogposts will load faster if you use Gutenberg to create them rather than Elementor. This is why we always suggest sticking with Gutenberg. A faster blog post will not only result in a better user experience, but it will also rank higher on Google.

The only applicable use case would be if you're creating a large blog post that contains many different design elements. An example of this type of post would be the interactive design posts that many news outlets publish on major events. For example, on New York Times they have their typical news articles (which has the featured image, title, content, and comments with limited design), but they also have interactive blogposts for major events. At the time of publishing, the New York times has a large interactive "page like" blog post for the coronavirus pandemic that shows visual statistics and more. That might be a good use of the Elementor page builder in a blog post, but for anything less than that, you should stick with Gutenberg.

Contact

The final page that we want to discuss building in this book is the contact page for your website. In most instances, the contact page for your small business website is the conversion page. This is the page that you're going to funnel all of your visitors to with your blog posts and pages like services. Once the visitor ends up on the contact page, they will enter their information, requesting a quote or more info on the services that you have to offer, and they will go from a visitor to an actionable lead.

In the best case scenario, your user will go from visitor to lead to paying customer.

Your website is one of the cheapest ways you can generate actionable leads. By funneling people to it, you'll know that those who submit contact forms are only interested in what you have to offer. Compared to paid ads, organically generated leads through your website convert more and also pay more. Also, depending on the services that you have to offer, a potential lead could value from a couple $100 to thousands of dollars. This is why getting the contact page right is essential.

We already discussed the best practices in a previous section in this book, but now let's talk about how to actually build your contact page.

Like any other page on the website, we're going to be using an Envato Elements template as a starting point. create a new WordPress page, load the Elementor editor, install the template on your contact page, and change all of the placeholder elements to match your company.

Most contact pages will include a place for you to have a Google map, address, and generic contact information. Additionally, most templates at least by Envato Elements do not contain contact forms. Having a contact form on your website is extremely important, so we're going to discuss how to create and add a contact form now.

First, you'll want to find a good place to put the contact form. In our template, we're going to replace placeholder text with the form.

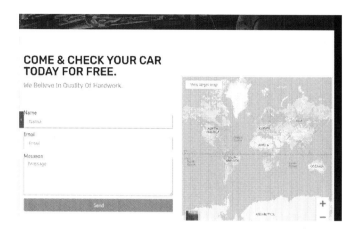

The default version of the contact form contains a field for your name, email and message. We recommend changing and adding fields depending on the information that your business needs to collect. Be sure to follow the best practices outlined in a previous section in this book.

The creation and configuration of the form is fairly straightforward. In the page builder interface, you can add remove and edit existing fields.

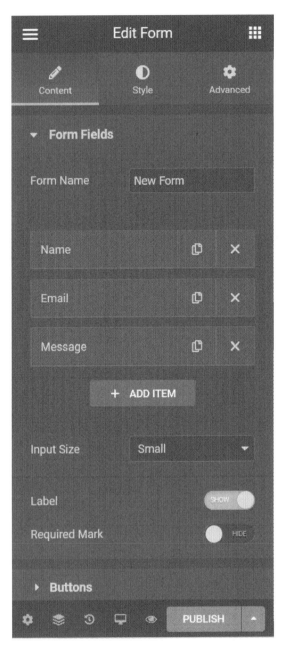

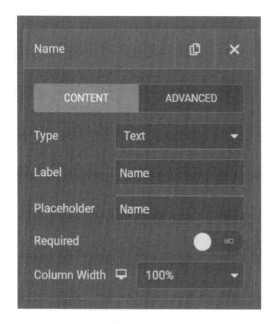

You can reorder fields by dragging them around in the page builder interface.

The choice of fields is immense, and you can collect any form of information that you may require, other than stripe or PayPal payments. If you do find yourself needing to collect payments, there are a few free plugins that will enable this functionality, though you may want to invest in a premium plugin dedicated to payment processing.

You can style your form by going to the style section of the Elementor builder, and changing colors, typography, font families and more.

Once you have your form looking the way you want it to, it is absolutely essential that you correctly set up the actions after submission. You have a lot of options here, but the most popular one is simply sending a message to your email when somebody submits the contact form.

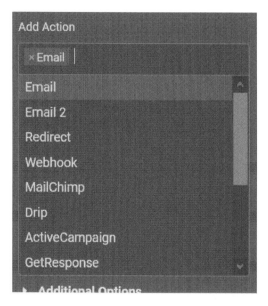

However, you can see that there are a lot of additional integrations, and this form builder is extremely powerful. You don't just need to use it for a contact form, instead you can use it to collect email addresses and put them on your mailing list, automatically send messages, and more.

In this use case, we're selecting email as our action after submission.

We're going to configure email to send to our info at email address, the subject is going to be new message from Elementor website and the message will contain all fields. Make sure that you configure the from email to be an email that contains the domain name that your website will go live on.

Right now, our website is hosted locally, and our domain name is https://localhost. Elementor will automatically assume that "localhost" is our live domain name and input it as the from email. We don't want this, as the sending mechanism won't properly work on a live host if this is the case. Instead, set this email to be the same sending email that you configured with SendInBlue.

When we bring our website live, we're going to test that this form works, but as long as the sending email address is the same one as your SendInBlue address, you should be good.

You can also set the form to send a second email notification to the submitter that notifies them that the form was successfully processed. You do this by adding a second email to the actions after submit, and configuring it to send to whatever email address was submitted in the form. We typically won't set this method up because the form displays a confirmation notice after successfully processing a submission, but there's an option to do this if you so desire.

One other thing we should mention is the fact that you can add as many actions after submission as you want. So, for example, you could add somebody to your mailing list, while emailing yourself a notification that somebody signed up. with this form, the possibilities are pretty endless, and you don't need to go out and purchase another form solution that would cost you anywhere from $49.00 to $99 per year.

Elementor also recently integrated multi step forms, which could be very helpful if you need to collect a large amount of information from your customer. We would recommend not using multi step forms on your contact page, but if you have a page where you need to collect a lot of customer information, splitting forms into multiple steps leads to higher conversion rates. For example, if you have somebody who is interested in carpet cleaning services, but you need to collect a lot of information about the room to accurately quote them, creating a multi step form with Elementor would be a great idea.

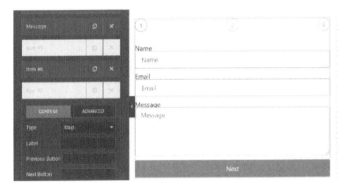

The one additional thing that you can do for your form is protected from spam. Contact form spam is a real thing, but it can be mitigated by implementing various protective methods.

The first thing you want to configure is a honeypot. A honeypot is a field that is invisible to humans, but visible to bots. If this field gets filled out by a bot, the form submission mechanism will be disabled and the spambot will not be able to send you any message.

If a human submits your form, the honeypot fields will not even be visible to them and this admission will be successful.

Read more about honeypot fields here:

https://www.thryv.com/blog/honeypot-technique/

You can also configure googles reCAPTCHA Which is an industry standard spam protection device.

This involves creating a free API key and installing it into your website. Elementor Pro allows you to easily do this by copying and pasting a public and secret key into two fields and hitting an input button. We're not going to dive into depth about incorporating the recapture device onto your contact form, but if you want to read more check out this knowledgebase article:

https://docs.Elementor.com/article/254-recaptcha

Sometimes, recapture will block real humans, which may result in lost revenue. In our opinion, the honeypot method works very well, blocks pretty much all spam that isn't human, and doesn't incorporate the third party reCAPTCHA service which not only slows down your website speed, but makes it difficult for real humans to submit forms sometimes. This is why will only incorporate reCAPTCHA if there is a big spam problem on the website in general.

The vanilla version of Elementor and Elementor Pro does not contain a form database. What this means is that form entries will only be emailed to you, and they won't be stored on your website. If you've used other form processors in the past like Gravity Forms, you'll be familiar with the entry management system. Entries are stored and visible on the back end of the WordPress website. If you would like to add this functionality to your Elementor website, there's a super easy and simple to install plugin called **Elementor Contact Form DB.**

This is a free plugin and is installed into your website just like all of the other free plugins. Simply go to plugins, add new, search for that form database plugin, and click the install button.

There's no additional configuration necessary, when somebody submits your contact form, the database will collect them and display them in an admin page. This is a great redundancy in case your email mechanism fails to work, you won't be losing any form notifications which could result in new paying customers.

Additional Aspects

Adding additional business specific pages should definitely apply to your company. Your website shouldn't just consist of a homepage, A blog page, and a contact page, you want services and about pages, as well as industry specific pages. Understanding what pages to add if you don't have a good idea might be difficult, so looking at existing websites for inspiration is always a good idea.

On each individual page, you should always include a call to action directing visitors to your conversion device, Which, in most cases is the contact page of the website. Most of the templates that we've seen include call to actions on all pages, but if they don't, you should include your own call to action.

This section should have introduced you to creating a Elementor website, creating new pages, installing templates, editing templates, building a blog, and more. By now, you should find yourself with a fully functional Elementor website.

Bringing Your Site Live

Review Development Website

Once you're done building your development website, and you think that you're ready to begin offering it to your customers by migrating it to a live host, the first thing you should do is review it. Run through the entire website and make sure all of the content is correct, that there are no typos, that links lead to where they need to go, that buttons work, and that contact forms submit.

Try posting a new blog post and ensure that your archive page and blog post template are working.

Once you believe that your website is fully functional, and that all bugs and issues are resolved, have multiple other people look at it and run through the entire website. If you run a business, have some of your employees go through the website and see if they can find any errors or problems.

This is where local (this is the tool that we're using to host the development copy of the website on our individual computer) becomes really handy. You can create a temporary domain, which you can share too other people when requesting feedback. Let's go over how to create a temporary domain, share to other people, and request feedback.

On the main local dashboard, you will see a button that says enable live link.

If you click enable, it will generate a unique domain name that looks something like this: 9a7d0676fed5.ngrok.io

Until you delete the website or disable the live link (The live link will automatically disable itself in 12 hours, or stop functioning if you turn off your computer, or shut down local), this domain will be available on the public Internet.

When you enter this domain on any Internet browser, the public facing aspect of your website will load. You can explore this from multiple browsers, and multiple devices to see what your website will look like if you are a visitor of it.

You can also take this link an email and text it to coworkers, family, and friends, and request feedback. Requesting feedback from multiple people is a great way to identify any kinks or issues in the website. It'll also help you determine if everything is clearly written, and easy to use/navigate.

Keep in mind that this development domain is much slower to load then your final version of the website. This is just something that you should understand when sharing this website with others. once the website is on the final version of the hosting, we will optimize it for performance and speed, but at this point, you should only be focused on identifying major issues such as broken links, pages that aren't responsive on mobile devices, or poor usability.

Once you determine that your website is ready to move from the localhost to the live host, it's time to proceed. The first thing you need to do is set up your hosting.

Setting Up Hosting

We need to set up the server where your website files will be hosted on. When a visitor types in your domain name, files that are hosted on this server will be served to the visitor's browser, rendered, and displayed in the form of your website.

Cloudways is our recommended web host especially when it comes to Elementor installations. The service allows you to host your website on 1 of 5 industry-leading cloud provider platforms, like DigitalOcean or Vultr. Because you're leveraging these Cloud networks, you can get a lot of processing RAM, storage, and CPU power for less. Especially with an Elementor based website, you need a lot of processing power to ensure that it runs fast and performs well. The Cloudways platform sits on top of these Cloud providers and allows you to automatically provision new WordPress installations, install SSL certificates, run Security sweeps, and offers an easy-to-use interface between your server and you.

The server creation process in installation of WordPress is incredibly easy, and can be done in a few clicks. First, you'll want to sign up with a new account at Cloudways. If you use this link (https://isotropic.co/out/cloudways) and our agency code "ISOTROPIC" during sign up, you'll receive 30% off your first billing cycle. There's also a 30-day free trial, so you can test out the service before you even enter billing information. Unlike some other web hosts, this is a month-to-month billing set up, and they offer real time monthly billing estimates, as well as an aggregate end of the month estimate (3% margin of error).

Once you've signed up for your account, you can immediately create your server in these few steps.

This is the screen that you will be greeted with when you log into your platform for the first time. Click the green launch button to get started.

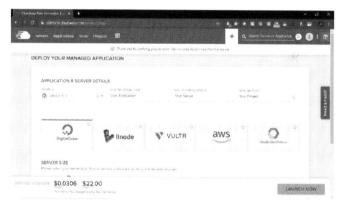

Now that you're here, the first thing to do is make sure you're installing the most up-to-date version of

WordPress. Then name your application, name the server, and name the project. This doesn't really matter and can be changed later.

You are presented with your options, which of the five leading Cloud providers. We recommend DigitalOcean for most installations. If you're interested in comparing and contrasting the five, we wrote a blog post on our agency blog that discusses the differences between the services: https://isotropic.co/breaking-down-cloudways-five-server-choices-for-wordpress-hosting/

For super simple WordPress installations, you can go for the $10 a month plan. This gives you 25 GB of hosting and 1 GB of memory, which is enough to make your Elementor website run quickly. If you have advanced features that require server-side processing like WooCommerce e-commerce, then you may want to opt for the $22 a month plan. Keep in mind that you can always scale up or down after installing WordPress on your server, in both processing power and storage size.

You can also install an unlimited amount of WordPress installations on your server, as long as they fit within your storage limitations. We recommend giving *at least* 1 GB of RAM to every WordPress installation.

Once you've selected your plan, this screen will show. It will say adding server for around seven minutes, and once the server is created you will be able to access both your WordPress installation and your new server.

There's a few other things that you can do like partitioning an SSL certificate, setting up SSH access and pointing a top-level domain to your server, but we'll discuss this in another blog post. If you can't wait, Cloudways offers 24/7 support 365 days a year, and they'll set it up for you!

One other thing that we like about the Cloudways setup for Elementor is that you can easily increase PHP memory values, and also upgrade your PHP version. Both of these functionalities are incredibly important for a fast and well performing Elementor website, and Cloudways delivers. Also, if you're working with a designer or a developer, you can give them access to your server without sharing your password. You can limit their access to the billing panel and allow them to only work with individual servers. This is incredibly helpful.

The reason we recommend the service is due to the sheer value it offers those running small to medium-sized websites. The live support, well designed platform, and ability to leverage Cloud Enterprise level hosting is a big plus for many. We also recommend it because it allows you to quickly and easily scale your processing power. For example, if your website suddenly balloons in size, you can quickly increase the storage capacity of the server. If you install woocommerce and need more memory, you can do this as well. This makes it so you don't need to migrate platforms which may be costly, and your on month-to-month billing, so there are no contracts to cancel. As you increase your usage, your bill increases as well.

Go check out Cloudways and take advantage of the free trial. Enter the code "ISOTROPIC" during sign up for 30% off your first billing cycle.

Connecting Your Domain

Now that your hosting is set up, it's time to connect your domain. If you don't have a domain, we're going to discuss how to acquire one in this next section. If you do have a domain, feel free to skip.

Getting A Domain

Our agency uses a service called Namecheap to purchase domains. Namecheap is, as its name suggests, fairly cheap, and easy to use.

We always recommend that you purchase a .com domain name. You may be tempted to go ahead and get a domain name like ".art" if you are an artist, something a bit outdated like ".net" or something that isn't standard like ".studio".

Getting anything other than a.com domain name is statistically proven to push visitors away and make your business look less credible. We always recommend getting a .com domain name, even when other domain names may look more appealing, and be cheaper.

A .com domain will typically cost you around at $9 per year. We like this service because it offers free identity protection. When you register a domain, you are required by law to give contact information. This information contains your email, name, address, and more. All of this information can easily be accessed via a database online.

The free identity protection service replaces your information with the Namecheap's information and ensures that you don't have any domain related contact information out there.

Purchasing the domain is very simple. All you need to do is go to their website, enter your domain name into their search bar on the home page, see if it's available, and hit the buy button. The company will try to upsell you on various products, but all you need is a domain name from them at this point.

For our example website, we've registered the domain name "**my-cool-biz-site-123.com**" through Namecheap. We will be connecting this domain name to Cloudflare, and our host, and then bringing our demo website live with it.

Using Cloudflare

Instead of directly connecting our domain from the registrar to Cloudways, we're going to use a third party servers called Cloudflare which will speed up our website, protect it from DDOS attacks, and help us manage our DNS records easily. It will also mask our IP address which makes our server installation more secure.

This is a very simple service to set up, and it's free which is why we included on all of our websites and recommended to everybody looking to connected domain name to a web host.

The first thing you need to do is sign up for a Cloudflare account. Once you have your account, it's time to set up your domain name with Cloudflare.

Clicking the add a side button will load a wizard in which you will be prompted to enter specific information such as the domain name, and the name of your website.

Accelerate and protect your site with Cloudflare

Enter your site (example.com):

my-cool-biz-site-123.com|

Add site

Want to add multiple sites? Learn how.

For what we're trying to do, the free plan is more than adequate. It offers you basic protection, basic performance acceleration, and a very easy to use DNS dashboard (the DNS management aspect of Cloudflare is the main reason that we incorporate it on all of our websites).

Once you've added the domain name, cloud waves will automatically find all DNS records associated with it, and add it to its interface.

Once you confirm all the records and hit the next button, Cloudways will give you two nameserver addresses which you will need to add to your domain via the registrar. In our case, we have registered our domain through Namecheap. Additional registrars maybe Google domains and GoDaddy. Like we said before, Namecheap is the cheapest platform out there, and it offers the best dashboard which is why we use it and recommended to all of our clients.

← Back

Change your nameservers

🛈 Pointing to Cloudflare's nameservers is critical for activating your site successfully. Otherwise, Cloudflare is unable to manage your DNS and optimize your site.

1. Log in to your Namecheap account

Remove these nameservers:

```
dns1.registrar-servers.com
dns2.registrar-servers.com
```

2. Replace with Cloudflare's nameservers:

 Nameserver 1

```
adaline.ns.cloudflare.com
```

Click to copy

 Nameserver 2

```
rocco.ns.cloudflare.com
```

Click to copy

Check to make sure they're correct, then **Save your changes.**

Registrars typically process nameserver updates within 24 hours. Once this process completes, Cloudflare confirms your site activation via email.

Learn how to change nameservers in Cloudflare.

Done, check nameservers

You can see that cloud flare identifies the pre-existing nameservers, and tells you to replace them with their own. Copy and paste both nameservers from Cloudflare, and navigate to your Namecheap domain dashboard.

Under the Namecheap domain dashboard, find your domain name, and click the manage button to the right previewed in our case, we have multiple domains registered under this account, so we need to find our domain out of the list of dozens. In your case, this may be the only domain you have registered, so it's fairly easy to find.

Once you're in the domain management dashboard, find the nameservers section. It should be the third or fourth tab depending on the domain servers you have purchased.

By default, the name servers will be named cheap basic DNS, and you need to change these to the two servers that Cloudflare offers. From the drop down menu, change Namecheap basic DNS to custom DNS.

Copy and paste the Cloudflare nameservers into the DNS , and hit the check button. It may take up to 24 hours for these changes to take effect, but this typically occurs within the hour.

go back to the cloud player setup page, and click the done check nameservers button.

You can keep all of the default settings on the "**Set up security and speed configurations for your website**". Then, click done.

You'll need to wait anywhere from a couple minutes to up to 24 hours for the nameserver changes to take effect. Once the changes take effect, Cloudflare will send you an email.

Connect Domain To Your Host

Once you receive your email that the Cloudflare nameservers have propagated, it's time to connect the domain to your Cloudways host.

If cloud flare imported the default DNS settings that Namecheap applies to the domain upon purchase, your records should look something like this:

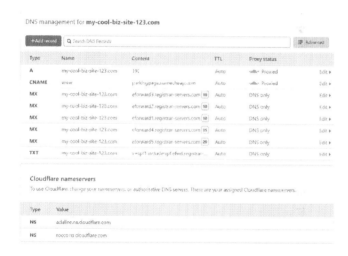

To connect the domain to the Cloudways host, we need to delete the CNAME record, and change the A record's IP address to match the IP address of our Cloudways server.

DNS management for **my-cool-biz-site-123.com**

Type	Name	Content	TTL	Proxy status	
A	my-cool-biz-site-123.com	192	Auto	Proxied	Edit ▾

Type	Name	IPv4 address	TTL	Proxy status
A	my-cool-biz-site-123.com	YOURSERVERIP		Proxied

Click on the individual A record, and update the IP address to match the Cloudways server IP address.

You can find your IP address for the Cloudways server by going to the platform dashboard, and clicking on the server tab.

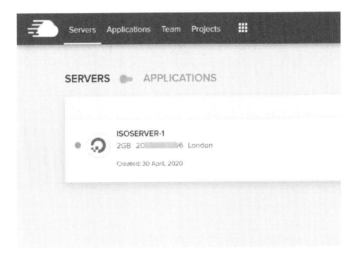

Find the server that will be hosting your website, in your case it is probably only a single entry, and next to the memory allocation underneath the title of the server, you'll be able to copy and paste your IP address.

For us, our server IP address is something like this:

20X.XX.XXX.XX6

We will then copy and paste this IP address into our Cloudflare a record. Save the A record, and the domain will now point to your server.

The next step is configuring the domain to connect to your actual application. Under the applications tab on the Cloudways platform, find your application (the term application also means WordPress installation in this implementation) name and click on the entry.

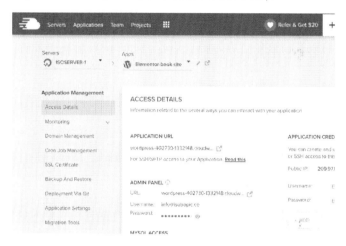

On this screen, click on the domain management tab. Under the domain management tab, enter your businesses domain as the primary domain entry.

If you need any help throughout this process, cloud Waze offers 24/7 live support for free. Instead of doing this yourself, you can request a support agent to do it for you, or at least help you walk through it.

Now, if you navigate to your business's domain name in any browser, it should be connected to a default WordPress installation.

If you see a screen like this, you have successfully connected your domain name to your hosting account. Now it's time to migrate your website from its local development environment to its live hosting environment.

Migrating To Your Live Host

To migrate the website away from the local development environment to the live host, we're going to be using a plugin called All-In-One WP migration. It's free, automatically changes your domain and works very well.

This is a simple, one click tool that will export your website in a package. You can then reinstall the website on any installation of WordPress by simply uploading the file and clicking import.

Before your migration

You want the PHP version of the old website and the new installation to be the same & you also want the WordPress version to be the same as well, as this will minimize any migration issues that you might have. Also, whatever you do, do not delete the existing website without completely migrating to the new website and testing that everything works.

You'll also want to follow the best practices of migrating your website. Ensure that everything is ready to go before you export your site — this means you'll need to be able to login to the new website, make sure everything functions on the site and more.

A big issue that we encounter is reCAPTCHA locking users out of their migrated websites. Many of the time, this plugin or additional security plugins will not allow you to log into the new installation of your website (upon import, you will be required to sign into the new site).

Our recommendation is to always disable every single plugin related to login/security that your website is using, and then re-enable that plugin upon migration.

That means that you should deactivate the WordFence plugin from the back end of your locally developed website. Do this by going to plugins, finding WordFence, and clicking the disable button.

We haven't had any issues with licenses failing to renew or function on migrated websites — this is because you're basically making a direct copy of your website, just putting it on a new server.

Migrating your website with this free tool is extremely simple. You export the .wpress file from your old site location to your desktop, and then simply re-upload that same file to the place you would like to migrate your website to.

To do this, go to the export tab of the plugin, click the "export to" button, and select file. It will begin creating and downloading a file onto your computer. That file will contain your word press website, and all the files that make it up.

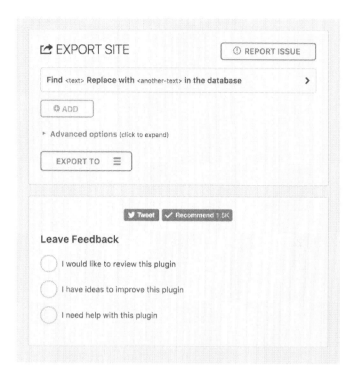

On the base installation of WordPress that is now present at your business domain, you need to log in and install the same plug into that website.

You can access your login credentials from the Cloudways platform. Simply navigate to the application, and on the initial loading screen, you'll be able to access your username and password.

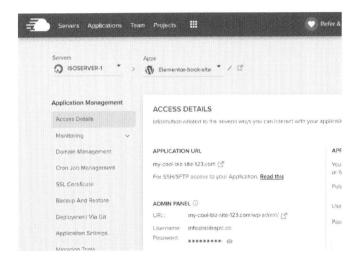

Under the admin panel section, copy and paste the URL into a new tab. Then copy and paste the username and password into the login interface, and enter your website. Install the all-in-one WordPress migration plugin in the same way that you installed it on your development website.

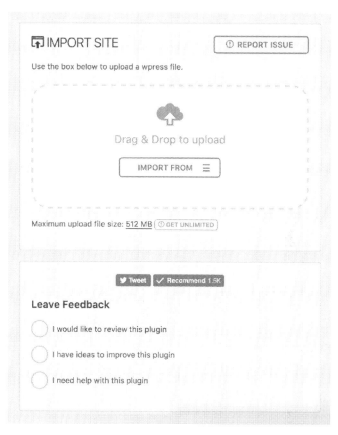

On the import side tab of the plugin, drag and drop the .wprss file that was downloaded onto your computer by the local installation of your WordPress website.

Begin the import process and in a matter of minutes your existing base WordPress installation will be replaced by a copy of your development website.

This plug-in will automatically change all URLs in your newly migrated website, to the URL of the existing receiving WordPress installation.

Now, if everything went according to plan your locally developed a website should be migrated to your live host. Go to your business domain, and ensure that the URLs were properly rewritten, and that the migration worked successfully.

At this point, your website will be live and publicly accessible. We recommend sharing it to friends and coworkers again and making sure that no links or functionality broke during the migration process.

Setting Up SEO Tools

Now that your website is live and publicly accessible by everyone from your customers to the Google search engine algorithm robots, it's time to optimize your website for maximum visibility.

There are several plugins that will help you optimize your website for SCO placement. We recommend a plugin called Rank Math.

Rank Math is a free plugin that can be installed via the WordPress plugin repository. go to plugins, add new, search for Rank Math, and install it. Once installed, Rank Math will display a setup wizard. Fill out the wizard and all the information in it.

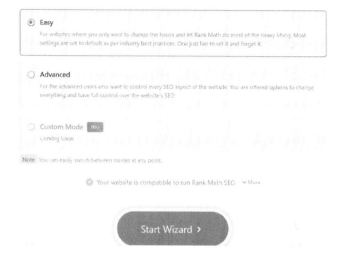

From the information that you input, this plugin will automatically optimize your website for search engine optimization, ranking placement, and more. It will add several lines of code to the header of your blog that will help Google search engine robots identifier. The plugin is pretty intuitive to use and set up.

Once the plugin is set up through the wizard, it's time to optimize every individual page that you have created for maximum search engine visibility. This isn't a necessary step of website creation, but doing it will lead to more traffic in more leads. It only takes a few minutes, so it's definitely worth it.

Go to the pages tab in your WordPress back end interface. Click on the individual page that you want to optimize with the Rank Math plugin. For this example, we're going to be using the home page.

In the upper right hand corner, you're going to see a SEO score. Clicking on that score will load the Rank Math plugin interface which you can use to optimize your page.

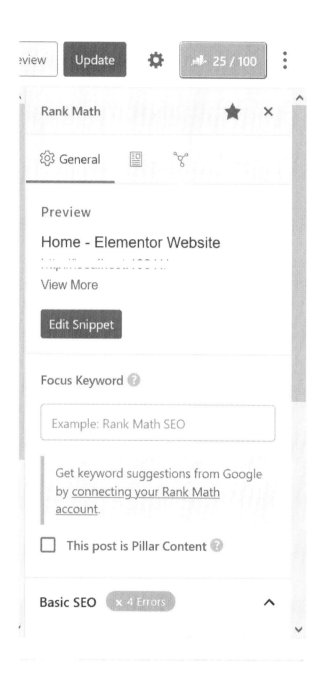

It will identify any SEO errors on your page and help you fix them. The highest score you can get is a 100 out of 100, and if you fix all the issues that Rank Math identifies, you will most likely rank high for your respective Google search keyword.

Repeat this process for every page and blog post on your website.

Ensuring Everything Is Working

Now, it's time to ensure that everything is working on your website once again. You should run through every page and blog post and make sure that all links are working and pointing to where they need to go. This is especially important after migration, because in very rare cases the links will not automatically be replaced with the live domain.

You should also share this with other people and get third party feedback on everything from usability to design to content to any issues they may find.

This is the final version of your website that will be served to customers, so you want to make sure that every aspect of it is professional, builds credibility, and eventually leads to more lead generation.

Optimizing Your Site

The final step of bringing your website live is optimizing it for performance and speed. Performance and speed directly impact your pages placement on the Google search rankings, and it also impacts the user experience. If a website takes over 3 seconds to load, 50% of the visitors will click away from it, so ensuring that your website loads as quickly as possible is very important.

There are many individual things that you can do for your website, but the two most important things to do is automatically optimize all images, and install a caching plugin that will allow your website to load faster for visitors by compressing files, and storing copies of them on the visitor's browser.

The first speed performance plug-in that we're going to be installing is called Breeze. Breeze is a caching plugin that is created by Cloudways and designed to work with their service.

Cloudways may have automatically installed this plug-in onto your WordPress website, but if they didn't it's free and installed via the WordPress repository. Go to the plugins page, search for the plugin, and click the install button.

Breeze – WordPress Cache Plugin

Breeze is a WordPress Caching Plugin developed by Cloudways. Breeze uses advance caching systems to improve WordPress loading times exponentially.

By Cloudways

Install Now

More Details

Once installed, go to the settings page for the plugin and enable the caching and file minification .

Cache System	This is the basic cache that we recommend should be kept enabled in all cases. Basic cache will build the internal and static caches for the WordPress websites.
Purge cache after:	1440 Automatically purge internal cache after x minutes. By default this is set to 1440 minutes (1 day).
Minification	☑ HTML
	☑ CSS
	☑ JS
	☑ Include inline JS
	☑ Include inline CSS
	Check the above boxes to minify HTML, CSS, or JS files. Note: We recommend testing minification on a staging website before deploying it on a live website. Minification is known to cause issues on the front-end.
Gzip Compression	☑ Enables this to compress your files making HTTP requests faster and faster.
Browser Cache	☑ Enable this to add expires headers to static files. This will tell browsers to either re-load a file from server or fetch from the browser's cache.
Enable cache for logged-in users	☐ Enable this for WP founders with roles: Administrator, Editor, Author, Contributor. Note: This option might not work properly with some page builders.

We recommend checking off every setting on the first page other than caching for an admin account.

Under advanced settings, you can opt to group both CSS and JavaScript files.

When enabling these features, you need to consistently check the front end (multiple pages, not just the home page) to see if this breaks anything. In some cases, merging and minifying JavaScript files will break the functionality of the website. You need to make sure that this doesn't happen, because a fast website that's broken is just as bad as a slow website that isn't.

Once the cash is properly enabled and in place, your website will load much faster than before.

Now, it's time to install a plugin that will allow you to automatically optimize images. Optimizing images resizes them, and compresses them so there is less data transferred when the page is called. This ultimately results in a faster page speed loading time for your end visitor.

For this, we use a plugin called Imagify:

Imagify – WebP & Image Compression and Optimization

Install Now

More Details

Optimize images in one click: reduce image file sizes, convert WebP, keep your images beautiful... and boost your loading time and your SEO!

By WP Media

Once installed, follow the setup wizard and create a free account.

Image optimization is a very resource intensive task, so doing it on your server is not a good idea. The reason you need to create an account and get an API key is because this service offloads the image optimization to its own servers. In essence, it takes the images on your website, resizes them on their own servers using their own processing power, and then re downloads the images unto your website.

If you have a small website, this service is free (You get up to 25 Milla bytes of image optimization per month for free), but if you have a bunch of photos, you will need to pay for API access. Luckily, this is fairly cheap ($4/month), and will make a noticeable difference in the page speed loading time.

Once you create your account and install your API key, you can simply click a button that says bulk optimize images, and optimize all of the images on your website to load as quickly as possible.

We also offer a professional WordPress speed optimization service over at speedopp.com if you want to get professional help in this arena.

Congratulations, if you're at this point in the book, you should have a fully functional, as the own performance optimized website that is ready to be viewed by your clients. At this point, you can go from the development stage of your website to the maintenance stage of your website.

Maintaining & Growing Your Site

Maintenance

Because you build your website with Elementor, it's easy to keep the design styling of the website up to date. A big turnoff to many potential customers is if your website looks outdated. For example, your company will lose credibility in the eyes of a visitor if the website looks outdated.

You should also check your website every few weeks and ensure that all plugins and WordPress versions are up-to-date. Making sure that your plugins in WordPress versions are up-to-date ensures that there will be no security vulnerabilities that hackers can use to gain access to your website.

When you check your website, manually run a WordFence scan and ensure that your website is clean of any malicious code.

Also, if you're using the Elementor form database, check it and make sure all form notifications have been dealt with via email. If you see a bunch of form entries in the database, but haven't received email notifications, your email system isn't working properly and you need to fix it.

Ongoing SEO

If you have a good looking, well designed, high performing website, You should already be reaping the rewards from it. Visitors who end up on the website are impressed by the professionalism that your company offers, your businesses credibility is increased, and your website is happily generating leads. However, to make the most out of your new digital presence, doing on going SEO is a great idea, and will net you a positive return on investment.

The key to on going SEO is signifying to Google that you are publishing high quality content that is valuable to readers, and that your website is active and not abandoned. The best way to do this is to publish A blog post article every week that offers high quality content that visitors actually want to read. If you publish an article every read, it signifies to Google that your website is active, and offers readers valuable information. Google will incorporate this into their search engine algorithm, and your website will likely place higher for keywords. you can also incorporate keyword research, and target high value low competition keywords, which would ensure the 1st, second or third place on the Google search results for your individual blog post. This would lead to more inbound traffic, giving more domain authority, give you more knowledge authority, and increase the credibility of your company.

In most cases, you don't need to be paying anybody hundreds of dollars per month for SEO, especially if you're website was not previously an essential aspect to your company. In our opinion, most SEO services are a waste of your money, and you would be better off spending this money on paid search engine placement (see below).

On the topic of lead generation, now that you have a properly functioning, and well-designed website, you may want to throw your hat in the ring with paid advertisements. Purchasing a couple $100 of Google or Facebook advertisements, or hiring a marketing agency to do this for you might be a good experiment this see if running paid advertising campaigns will increase your revenue.

We recommend thinking about paid advertisements after your website has proven to be a good lead generation with inbound marketing only. If you know that your website will generate leads organically, so a visitor ends up on your website via referral or something like that, and they end up becoming a customer from it, then pushing visitors to your website with paid advertising may be a great idea and net a positive return on investment.

Conclusion

We hope that this book was beneficial in helping you create a WordPress website with Elementor for you or your small business. The principles and resources outlined in this book are used by our design agency in our everyday development and website creation processes.

If you have any questions regarding building an element or website, feel free to join one of our respective Facebook (or Reddit) groups, or reach out via email:

The Digital Presence Mastermind:
https://www.facebook.com/groups/digitalpresencemas termind/

ElementorQA (Questions & Answers):
https://www.facebook.com/groups/264645379212724 4/

SiteSpeed (Speed Optimization) subreddit:
https://reddit.com/r/sitespeed

You can also find many resources regarding WordPress design/development, and website speed/performance on our blog at: https://Isotropic.co/blog/.

Resource Directory:

Services & Websites

Name	Description	Link	Additional Info
Cloudways	Cloudways is our recommended webhost due to their value for money and ease of use.	https://elementorqa.com/cloudways	Use code "ISOTROPIC" for 30% off your first month of hosting.
Namecheap	Namecheap is our recommended domain name registrar due to their low pricing	https://isotropic.co/out/namecheap/	

	an easy to use platform.		
Cloudflare	Cloudflare protects your website from DDO S attacks and offers a place for you to easily manage DNS records for free.	Cloudflare.com	
Isotropic Design	isotropic design is the digital agency behind this book. If you were	Isotropic.co	

	looking for any website design or development that falls outside of your scope, feel free to reach out.		
Speed Opp	speed up is a professional speed optimization service that guarantees a website home page loading time of three	SpeedOpp.com	

	seconds or less.		
Elementor QA	Elementary QA is a forum website where you can ask and answer any questions you may have about the Elementor page builder.	ElementorQA.com	
Official Elementor Facebook Group	Perfect for Elementor support.	https://www.facebook.com/groups/Elementors/	

Plugins

Name	Description	Link	Additional Info
Breeze	Caching & speed optimization.	https://wordpress.org/plugins/breeze/	
WordFence	WordPress security.	https://wordpress.org/plugins/wordfence/	
Rank Math	Search engine optimization.	https://wordpress.org/plugins/seo-by-rank-math/	
Envato Elements	Additional templates for Elementor Pro.	https://wordpress.org/plugins/envato-elements/	
SendIn Blue	SMTP transactional email.	https://wordpress.org/plugins/mailin/	
Elementor Pro	Page/theme builder.	https://isotropic.co/out/elementor	
Imagify	Image optimization.	https://wordpress.org/plugins/imagify/	

Printed in Great Britain
by Amazon